AGAINST!

AGAINST!

REBELLIOUS DAUGHTERS IN BLACK IMMIGRANT FICTION IN THE UNITED STATES

Asha Jeffers

THE OHIO STATE UNIVERSITY PRESS
COLUMBUS

Copyright © 2025 by The Ohio State University.
All rights reserved.

Library of Congress Cataloging-in-Publication Data
Names: Jeffers, Asha, author.
Title: Against! : rebellious daughters in Black immigrant fiction in the United States / Asha Jeffers.
Description: Columbus : The Ohio State University Press, 2025. | Includes bibliographical references and index. | Summary: "Examines US fiction focused on African and Afro-Caribbean immigrant and second-generation daughters to better understand how national identity and gender inform rebellion. Considers works by Paule Marshall, Edwidge Danticat, Chimamanda Ngozi Adichie, and Taiye Selasi, among others"—Provided by publisher.
Identifiers: LCCN 2024037353 | ISBN 9780814215791 (hardback) | ISBN 9780814283813 (ebook)
Subjects: LCSH: American fiction—African American authors—History and criticism. | American fiction—Women authors—History and criticism. | American fiction—20th century—History and criticism. | American fiction—21st century—History and criticism. | Daughters in literature. | Children of immigrants in literature. | Conflict of generations in literature. | African diaspora in literature. | Women, Black, in literature. | LCGFT: Literary criticism.
Classification: LCC PS153.B53 J44 2025 | DDC 813/.5409352996073—dc23/eng/20240921
LC record available at https://lccn.loc.gov/2024037353

Other identifiers: ISBN 9780814259337 (paperback)

Cover design by Alexa Love
Text composition by Stuart Rodriguez
Type set in Minion Pro

CONTENTS

Acknowledgments — vii

INTRODUCTION	Against!	1
CHAPTER 1	Rebelling in the In-Between	30
CHAPTER 2	Rebelling against Repetition	55
CHAPTER 3	Self-Destructive Rebellion	77
CHAPTER 4	Rebelling against Stereotypes and Confinement	105
CONCLUSION	The Future of Immigrant Blackness	130

Works Cited — 143

Index — 147

ACKNOWLEDGMENTS

First, I would like to thank my editor, Ana Maria Jimenez-Moreno, who so kindly and thoughtfully shepherded this manuscript through the publication process. Thanks to the many folks at OSU Press whose work contributed to the production of this book as well. I have immense gratitude toward my peer-reviewers. Your engagement with this work made it stronger.

This book was written at a particularly strange time in my life and in the world: during the first few years at a new institution, for which I had moved far from home, and during a global pandemic and its aftermath. I could not have managed either the teaching or the writing without the support of a great many people. I would like to thank my colleagues first at University of King's College and then at Dalhousie University, who were and are supportive and provided several opportunities to share aspects of this work as it was being written. Special shout-out to Roberta Barker, the best faculty mentor anyone could wish for. Thinking through this work in public was also very enriching; special thanks to my collaborators on the Daughters of Immigrants project, whose fellowship has been a wonderful product of a distinctly unwonderful time.

I am a remarkably lucky person in many ways, and one of those ways is that I have so many brilliant friends with whom to share and discuss my work. Marquita Smith was my most consistent and insightful reader; exchanging chapters with her meant getting excellent feedback and also getting to see a master at work. Andrew Brown was also an excellent chapter-exchange partner in the later stages of the project. My earliest reader, and one of the most important, encouraging, and beloved interlocutors and friends I have, was Vinh Nguyen, who also put me on to the work of the brilliant erin Khuê Ninh, which has had a significant effect on my work ever since. Not only is erin Khuê Ninh an incisive and compelling writer, but she is also a generous mentor and reader.

I have been lucky to receive the friendship and encouragement of too many people to list here, but I'm going to try anyway. Thank you to fellow scholars Anna P., Anna V., Ajay, Azar, Bart, Camille, Cat, Erin, Fayola, Gökbörü, Greg, Hilary, Kait, Ken, LiLi, Malissa, Maral, Meryl, Mike, Nadine, Nafisa, Nandini, Nicole, Phanuel, Sarah, Simon, Stephanie, Sylvia, Tim, Thy, and the late Y-Dang. Thank you to wise and worldly nonacademics Alyssa, Amina, Arden, Brendan, Dagna, Fazeela, Greer, Gunjan, Hiwot, Irfan, Keshia, Michelle, Nadia, Pacinthe, Rossana, and Stef.

For someone writing a book about rebellious daughters, I am a laughably unrebellious one. I could not have done this work and many other things without the incredible support of my family. The unwavering presence of my immediate family—my mother, Denise; my father, Francis; and my brothers, Adom and Chike—has held me up throughout my life. Thanks to Tina and Erin for their support and intelligence as well, and for being the mothers of the next generation: Aminata, Ayo, Aza, and Amara. This book is dedicated to the women who came before me, including Aunty Jessie, who taught me how to read; Grandma, whose love of writing inspired me; and Granny, whose life has taught me many lessons. This book is also dedicated to the memory of Donald Goellnicht.

INTRODUCTION

Against!

In Haitian American author Edwidge Danticat's *Breath, Eyes, Memory*, the protagonist's mother remarks about her daughter's baby, "She's a good child. . . . *C'est comme une poupée*. It's as if she's not here at all" (178). In this context, a "good" girl child is so quiet that you can forget that she is even there. She does not ask for anything, does not assert herself, does not ask to be seen or considered. The book you are reading is not about girls who are like dolls, girls who could be praised for seeming like they are not there at all. This book is about girls whose lives are shaped by forces of race, gender, migration, sexuality, family, and nation that are outside of their control and the various and sometimes strange tactics they use to resist and wrest control from these forces. This book explores the reoccurring theme of daughters who rebel in African and Afro-Caribbean immigrant and second-generation US fiction.

Intergenerational conflict is a common theme in immigrant fiction in general and is no less present in texts situated in the African diaspora. The ruptures that result from migration are particularly visible in the relationship between the generation who migrated and the one who was born or raised in the "elsewhere" to which the first arrived. Immigrant and second-generation writers mobilize these often-complicated familial relationships to comment on a variety of political, social, and psychic contexts. In particular, the prevalence of daughters who push back against patriarchal social and familial structures including gendered and classed expectations of behavior suggests that writers find this figure a particularly fruitful one through which they can examine how migration reshapes social relations. This book identifies the distinct but interconnected discourses of respectability and the model minority as the primary manifestation of these expectations and as the structures that characterize social relations in the afterlife of migration.

While the theme of familial conflict has been recognized and written about extensively in studies of Asian and Latina immigrant fiction, it has garnered less attention in studies of the African diaspora, a context that is significantly inflected by the way that race in general and Blackness specifically are constructed in the United States.[1] This gap in the scholarship is reflective of the overall lower emphasis on the familial in studies of the African diaspora, which perhaps speaks to the different way that African diasporic migrants are conceptualized more broadly: as solo sojourners, willing or unwilling, who lack strong family bonds. Yet the cultural production belies this view, showing Caribbean and African migrants to be enmeshed, sometimes much more than they would like, in meaningful and complex familial bonds and networks. An examination of these bonds and networks in all their ambivalence offers literary scholars the opportunity to shift away from an atomized view of the Black migrant to a more nuanced, psychologically rich understanding of migration and its aftereffects for members of the African diaspora, particularly women and girls.

This book is primarily concerned with "daughter" as a social position—a child who is defined by those around her by her dependence on caregivers and her designation as female and is socialized during her coming-of-age in ways that are shaped by these factors. As such, the focus is on those assigned female at birth. While these girls and women do not always conform to gendered expectations, the female characters I write about in this project are cisgender. Exploring the themes of this book through narratives about transgender girls or nonbinary people assigned female at birth would be a rich addition to this area of inquiry, though it is beyond the scope of this project.

Over the course of four chapters, I examine the fiction of Paule Marshall, Edwidge Danticat, Taiye Selasi, and Chimamanda Ngozi Adichie in order to analyze how each text represents the figure of the rebellious daughter, whether an immigrant herself or the daughter of immigrants, and how this rebellion is informed by race, gender, ethnicity, and migration status. Spanning Marshall's 1959 novel *Brown Girl, Brownstones* through Danticat's 1994 novel *Breath, Eyes, Memory* to Selasi's and Adichie's 2013 novels *Ghana Must Go* and *Americanah*,

---

1. One of the few texts that has sought to fill this gap is Lisa D. McGill's *Constructing Black Selves*, which focuses specifically on Caribbean immigrants and their children.

this book traces the literary representation of the rebellious Black immigrant daughter across over fifty years and examines texts that depict continental African and Afro-Caribbean immigrant groups.

By engaging with novels that depict the coming-of-age of the daughters of Black immigrants, I trace how their protagonists' subject formation relates to their adherence to or rebellion against familial, cultural, or national expectations in order to consider what the intersections of migration, racialization, and gender construction can tell us about each of these processes, especially as they converge in the immigrant family. I argue that Black immigrant and second-generation American women writers produce work that recognizes the specificity of African and African-diasporic immigrant experiences without deracinating them. That is, rather than categorizing Black migrants as either immediately fully integrated into an African American experience or seeing them as another category altogether that is unbound by race, these writers identify the unstable position of Black migrants within the American racial landscape. As such, these literary texts undermine racially essentialist readings of Black American experience and offer an excellent opportunity to trace the contours of the relationship between Americanization and racialization. In so doing, my approach affirms the value and specificity of African American experiences without accepting that the relationship between the terms *African* and *American* can only have one form. This book insists on providing a greater understanding of the diversity of Black American experiences because the narrowing of what Blackness means and can mean is a long-time tool of white supremacy. This work builds on the important interventions of Carole Boyce Davies, whose foundational work in a transnational approach to Black women's writing asserts the value of reading Black women's writing as "a series of boundary crossings" and who pointed out in 1994 that to "primarily identify Black women's writing with the United States is to identify with US hegemony" (4).[2] To read African and African-diasporic immigrant literature as connected but not wholly subsumed within African American literature is to respect the powerful genealogy that emerged in the United States, a genealogy that has deeply informed African-diasporic writing the world over, but also to assert the other genealogies with roots elsewhere, whose routes have led them to a fruitful but somewhat ambiguous place within the American literary scene.

---

2. In the thirty years since the publication of Boyce Davies's book, its insights have remained valuable. At the same time, the rise of continental African immigrant women writers in the US has taken place in the interim, producing new dynamics and raising new questions that I address in this book.

By foregrounding rebellious daughters particularly, I draw out a theme that is prevalent in immigrant and second-generation women's writing across racial lines to situate these texts in the wider corpus of immigrant and second-generation writing. The daughter of immigrants finds herself to be a lightning rod of myriad issues of race, gender, migration, family, and identity, and the tactics that she may choose to navigate these strikes are as complicated as the conditions that produce them. This book is not about the triumph of the rebellious Black girl over all that assails her; I seek to consider how rebellion itself is neither always good nor always bad but instead deeply circumstantial and that the modes of it can tell us interesting and unsettling things about what is being rebelled against.

In my readings of immigrant and second-generation girls' coming-of-age as coming-into-difference, a framing I will expand on below, I see the word *against* as a key metaphor. The power of the word *against* is that, unlike terms like *resistance* or *refusal*, it does not *only* signal the desire for distance. In common speech, *against* contains two seemingly contradictory connotations: to be against something can mean to reject it, "I am against the war," but it can also mean to bring something close, "I hold you against my body." These two directions are both encompassed in the word and create a powerful metaphorical ground for the dynamics this book explores. The rebellious daughter of immigrants may simultaneously find herself embodying both of these directions in relation to the immigrant family and to the society in which she lives. She may find that this space of the dual meaning of *against* is the only viable option for living; neither a complete rejection nor an unmediated intimacy can serve as a sustainable living space in the context of the oppressive forces directed toward her from either within the family or from the wider society.

Context

Migration from Africa and the Caribbean to the United States of America, both before and after it became known as such, has been an ongoing and complex affair. Forced migration through enslavement is of course the primary source of the long-standing African American community, which included enslaved people brought directly from Africa as well as the movement of enslaved people within the Americas. In the postslavery period, Black migration to the US increased, reaching a high point of 12,243 in 1924 (Kasinitz 24). Following this, however, Black migration was severely restricted through legislation like the 1924 National Origins Act, which established a quota system that "set the annual quota of any quota nationality at 2 percent of the number of foreign-born persons of that nationality already residing in the continental United States in 1890," and as a result, "approximately 82 percent of immigrant visas under this law were allotted to northern and western European countries, 16 percent to southern and eastern European countries and 2 percent to all other Eastern Hemisphere admissible nationalities" (Miyares and Airriess 36). Despite these restrictions, the foreign-born Black population and their American-born children reached 178,000 in 1930, although there was some reversal of this pattern during the Great Depression when more Caribbean immigrants returned to their former homes rather than arrived in the US (James 220). Nevertheless, these numbers are tiny compared to the overall migration during this period; almost 30 million immigrants arrived during this time. This information is meant to demonstrate just how drastically immigration patterns changed following the alteration of these explicitly racist laws.

The latter half of the twentieth century saw significant legal shifts that greatly increased the migration of Black immigrants. The 1952 Immigration and Nationality Act contained noteworthy changes from previous acts, such as the admissibility of all nationalities for US citizenship (Miyares and Airriess 37). This act was then amended in the Immigration Reform Act of 1965, the act which "finally eliminated national origin, race, ethnicity or ancestry as a basis for immigration" (Miyares and Airriess 39). As a result of this act and subsequent amendments, as well as the Refugee Act of 1980, the ethnic makeup of the migrant population altered dramatically. In the second decade of the twenty-first century, sub-Saharan Africans make up 4.5 percent of immigrants to the US, and this percentage is likely to grow, based on previous trends, as "between 2010 and 2018, the sub-Saharan African population increased by 52 percent, significantly outpacing the 12 percent growth rate for the overall foreign-born population during that same period" (Echeverria-Estrada and Batalova). Caribbean immigrants, meanwhile, have a longer history of being recruited as workers to the US in fields like agriculture and healthcare and currently make up 10 percent of the immigrant population.[3] While the Caribbean population is ethnically diverse, the majority are of African descent. According to the Pew Research Center, around 10 percent of the Black population in the US is made up of immigrants (Tamir). The exponential growth of African and Caribbean immigrants to the US has brought together multiple streams of the African diaspora in a context where the preeminent form of Blackness is African American in the sense of the descendants of enslaved Africans brought to the Americas in the sixteenth to the nineteenth centuries.

---

3. See Zong and Batalova for an overview of this history.

This confluence produces a particular set of circumstances that complicate simplistic views of racial categories and community identities. Many immigrants arriving from Africa have not previously had reason to consider themselves as "Black" but rather have other identity markers much more relevant to their lives, including national, regional, ethnic, religious, and community-based associations. As Boyce Davies notes, "'Blackness' is a color-coded, politically-based term of marking and definition which only has meaning when questions of racial difference and, in particular, white supremacy are deployed" (7). Migrants from the Caribbean generally arrive with a sense of Blackness, but it looks, sounds, and in numerous ways is different from the forms of African American identity they encounter upon their migration. At the same time, these migrants need to learn American racial politics very quickly upon their arrival, because regardless of how they might see their own identities, they are subject to American racial norms and ideologies. The purpose of this project is not to trace these sociological circumstances but rather to consider how four Black women writing throughout the twentieth and early twenty-first centuries creatively explored and responded to these forces.

Part of what this book lays bare is that "U.S. racial identity is a constructed legal fiction" and that

> racial identitarianism has an absolutely persistent political and social iteration that gains a substantive and familiar presence through its consistent and evolving engagements even, and especially, when these are fiction. However, rather than achieving some cognizable or visible coherence from a familiar black literary subjectivity, the evolving matter of identity comes to reflect the kind of destabilization that is notable in poststructuralist theory as it becomes a merely an evidentiary fragment in what is best understood as a vast postmodernist collage. (Holloway 5)

Black immigrant women writers demonstrate the stickiness as well as the instability of US racial identity through their work. As Holloway points out in the same study of law and African American literature, the law and Black identity in the US are inextricably linked because the law regulated the system of slavery that made race a matter of law (6). Because the way that race functions in the US is a direct result of slavery as a legal institution, the arrival of African and Afro-Caribbean immigrants into US racial politics creates a disorientation both within US racial discourses and in the immigrants themselves. Black immigrants' homelands have their own histories that, while deeply connected to the African American context through the shared history of colonialism, imperialism, slavery, and exploitation, have gone through different legal and, as a result, cultural transformations that produce different racial sensibilities. As Michelle M. Wright points out, there are three main types of historical placement of Africans to the West: "Those blacks brought into the 'home space' of the colonizer—African Americans—and those who were brought to a 'third space'—the Caribbean—in which neither blacks nor whites originally understood that space as their 'home'" as well as "a third type of placement, namely Black Africans being colonized within their own home space by European military, political, and economic power" (7). These types signify differences not only in "chronological placement, physical placement, and the racial discourses in each that sought to interpellate them" but "in the ways they have subverted, resisted, or otherwise reacted against those discourses" (7). Each distinct context shapes life and consciousness in significant ways.

Added to these differences is the nonrepresentative nature of immigrant populations, meaning that immigrants in general do not reflect the entirety of their home country's population. Immigrants generally come from "striving" sections of society, both because of government policies that offer visas to people with particular skills and education levels as well global dynamics of development and underdevelopment that see many of the most ambitious and most educated from the Global South emigrating for more opportunities (Nnaemeka 134). The racial sensibilities of these types of immigrants are also shaped by class dynamics that are deeply tied to race in their countries of origin. In the Caribbean, the expectation that class ascendancy can overcome positions of racial oppression became sufficiently ingrained so that Caribbean immigrants found themselves unprepared for the realities of racial hierarchies in their sites of settlement:

> the tradition of viewing cultural values and modes of behavior associated with British middle-class society as a sign of high social standing meant that the migrants who traveled to Western destinations had a strong expectation that these societies would provide the opportunity to earn a position as respectable citizens if only they were ambitious and hardworking. They were not prepared for the discriminatory racial and ethnic regimes in the migration destinations, and this had an important impact on the ways they, and their descendants, perceived themselves as possible citizens in the receiving society and their Caribbean society of origin. (Olwig 30)

Of course, Caribbean people of African descent were not unfamiliar with racial hierarchies, but they were indoctrinated into a colonial discourse of class that downplayed the centrality of race in one's social position. Olwig argues that the idea of "respectability" came to stand in for all of the values and behavioral patterns encouraged by the British, ways of seeing and being that were "an ideal of citizenship that became an important ideological basis of post-emancipation colonial society, and thus of individual and economic mobility" (29). Respectability is, therefore, understood to be tied to both British and middle-class identity. These ways of seeing and being were the source of a sense of power for African Caribbean people at the very same time as they were damaging.

Concurrently, immigrants regardless of race enter into a US racial hierarchy that consistently puts African Americans at the bottom, which encourages immigrants to distance themselves from African Americans as much as possible. Because of the ways that various groups are racialized in America, this encouragement and the reaction to it can look a variety of different ways, but the imperative remains the same. Much has been written about autoethnography in immigrant fiction, but a great deal less has been written about the ethnographic gaze of the immigrant into the site of settlement. All immigrants are amateur ethnographers. The imperative to observe and understand comes from the need to put into practice the knowledge such observations produce: social expectations, common expressions, warnings signs for violent or difficult interactions. They must observe the culture and politics of the place where they are settling in order to survive and to thrive. Because white supremacy is the underpinning force of American society, immigrants often take it on either consciously or subconsciously in order to better their chances at building the life they aim to have. Of course, buying into white supremacy is damaging in a variety of ways. There is the moral damage of taking part in a corrupt system, but on a more personal level, accepting the racial hierarchy as it stands means also accepting one's own lower-status place in it, even if that puts one ahead of some others. Nevertheless, immigrants, including those from Africa and the Caribbean, often take on anti-Black racism as a part of the price of admission.

This acceptance of the racial hierarchy produces an obvious problem for Black immigrants: how can they both accept the anti-Blackness required of them by the nation and gain the advantages that are promised them, advantages that are made possible by anti-Blackness that also affects them despite their desire to distance themselves from African Americans? In other words, they are expected to set themselves up against African Americans while they cannot help but be aware of the closeness between their positions; here we see a concrete example of the duality of againstness. An Ethiopian shop owner, for example, may follow African American shoppers around his store and then find himself receiving the same treatment at Walmart. Much representation of Black immigrants portrays this paradoxical position. This representation is particularly potent when it demonstrates the tensions between immigrants and their children, as the immigrant generation seems more able to maintain their own sense of difference while the children of immigrants, socialized in the US context, are better able to recognize the ways that this devil's bargain of anti-Blackness fails to achieve its expected ends. This clarity can lead to promising visions and practices of solidarity between Black immigrants, or at least their children, and African Americans.

The discursive role of the immigrant in the nation more generally is based on expedience and, as a result, changes significantly over time and place. The nation-states of the West have often found that immigrants, along with their economic usefulness, can serve as symbols of an outside that can either be benevolently let in or heroically kept out in order to maintain the "true nature" of the national culture. Paul Gilroy notes,

> It is not, as many commentators suggest, that the presence of immigrants corrodes the homogeneity and solidarity that are necessary to the cohesion and mutuality of authentically social-democratic regimes, but rather that, in their flight from socialistic principles and welfare state inclusivity, these beleaguered regimes have produced strangers and aliens as the limit against which increasingly evasive national particularity can be seen, measured and then, if need be, negatively discharged. (xxxiii)

The pathologizing of the immigrant family in media and political discourse serves an important role in this project. The children of immigrants are set up as a site of contestation between the supposed national culture and the suspicious foreignness of the immigrant parents. Will the immigrant child "choose" to become one of "us" or will she remain an outsider like her parents? If she becomes one of us, our superiority is demonstrated. If she does not, our suspicions were justified. Thus, the immigrant daughter's rejection of the family or the family's practices can be appropriated by the larger society to represent the goodness and modernity of the mainstream. Sara Ahmed identifies how this view has been perpetuated through media so that "the unconventional daughter of the migrant family might even provide a conventional form of social hope" (138). In this way, the lives of immigrant daughters can be mobilized for discourses that cast immigrants as perpetual outsiders who must be altered in order to belong.

Many Black immigrant women writers consistently try to resist this appropriation in their writing. The delicate space in which they work, whereby criticism of the family can be used to shore up ideologies and practices that do not serve their best interests at the same time as the silencing of intrafamilial oppressive dynamics can be used to support systems and social structures that are also damaging, leads Black immigrant women writers to be very self-conscious about the politics of representation. How to represent a philandering father, for example, without reinforcing the hypersexualization of Black men, or to represent a long-suffering mother without reproducing the idea of the "strong black woman"? The question of how to write the complexities and even ugliness within immigrant families without playing into stereotype yields a variety of answers from different writers. Of course, this question is not unique to Black immigrant women writers; the antipathy between Zora Neale Hurston and Richard Wright shows clearly that recent migration need not be a factor in the debate over representing Black people's "dirty laundry." Yet the particularities of how immigrants are discursively positioned heavily inflect this conversation.

There is also significant diversity in terms of how various Black immigrant groups are perceived in the public imaginary, for a variety of reasons. In the context of this book, I begin by engaging with two Black Caribbean immigrant and second-generation novels and then move on to explore two continental African immigrant and second-generation novels. In the early twentieth century, Anglophone Caribbean immigrants like those depicted in *Brown Girl, Brownstones* were perceived through a more explicit model minority–style lens than they would come to be later in the century. Haitian immigrants, on the other hand, were and are subject to more consistently negative associations, as Danticat addresses in *Breath, Eyes, Memory*. In contrast to both of these Caribbean contexts, Nigerian and Ghanaian immigrants like those depicted by Selasi and Adichie are much more positively perceived, as they are often understood as arriving under professional visa categories or as university students. This is not to say that all continental African immigrants are viewed in the same way; African migrants who arrive as refugees are often more ambivalently positioned. Despite these significant differences, the novels reveal the consistent presence of both immigrant striving for upward mobility and status as well as rebellious daughters who resist familial and social expectation.

Respectability and the Model Minority

The early twenty-first century saw the rise of a public conversation on the topic of "respectability politics," the idea that marginalized groups are expected to adhere to more rigorous standards of civility and morality than members of dominant groups in order to be afforded basic rights and considerations.[4] This idea has been rightly criticized because engaging in respectability politics tacitly accepts that marginalized people are responsible for proving their worthiness or even humanity to the dominant group and that failing to do so justifies their mistreatment. I am interested not in whether this demand to prove worthiness is right or wrong (it is wrong), but rather why respectability politics are so powerful despite the obvious flaw in their logic. As Susana Morris points out, "respectability politics . . . grows out of a complicated and intertwined set of political histories and prerogatives that are concerned with improving conditions for Blacks but that also employ tactics such as surveillance, control, and repression; that provide insufficient political gains; and that ultimately secure the hegemony of ruling social structures" (8). In other words, respectability shores up the structures it is meant to protect against.

At the same time, many people have just as correctly pointed out that refusing to abide by respectability politics does not remove the social structures that produced this coping mechanism in the first place. In the case of immigrants, expectations of respectability are colored by the widespread if often implicit belief that immigrants are meant to be proving themselves to the nation; they are an "unnatural" presence that becomes naturalized legally but also through their behavior. Their conformity to social norms, displays of gratitude and patriotism, and economic success justify their admittance into the nation-state. Morris notes that this impulse has intertwined economic and social roots: "Respectability politics reflects a marked, though often futile, desire for social mobility, and the notion that class advancement is based on cultural assimilation to the norm is at the heart of much public discourse in both the Caribbean and the United States" (13). For immigrants from the Caribbean, the game of class ascendency through respectability is already a familiar one before their arrival in the United States. As many have pointed out, the respectability of women and girls is particularly scrutinized. What this scrutiny looks like varies based on a complex map of social values; a Muslim woman who wears hijab and a Dominican woman who wears booty shorts can both be seen as contravening the rules of respectability because the standard is not actually about how covered or uncovered a body is but rather what the body signifies.

Because respectability is defined by forces beyond Black women's control, their ability to fulfill its demands are not guaranteed. Morris lays out the paradox of respectability, which she describes as "simultaneously desiring to

---

4. The term "the politics of respectability" was coined by Evelyn Brooks Higginbotham in 1993 to describe the activities that have come to be more often phrased as respectability politics.

be respectable according to the ideals of respectability politics and finding this difficult, if not impossible" because "respectability, at least as imagined through the current manifestation of the politics of respectability, is largely out of reach for many Blacks, which makes being judged by or internalizing a rubric informed by these politics unfair at best and cruel at worst" (3). Respectability can be both actively desired and unattainable for Black women, whose conditions of life fundamentally do not line up with the middle-class, Eurocentric ideologies that are the source of North American ideals of respectability.

The purpose of identifying the unattainability of respectability is to demonstrate its flawed nature. Morris contends that Black women writers do not write about this paradox to pathologize the Black family but rather to critique the paradox itself; she argues that

> there is a discernable tradition in Black women's literature from the Caribbean and the United States written in the last decades of the twentieth century that challenges many popular discourses around the concepts of family and respectability and that advocates for radical understandings of community support and accountability, especially as these relate to women's roles within families. (4)

In my work on the literature of the children of immigrants, I have always prioritized moving away from a model that pathologizes feelings of unbelonging and intergenerational conflict because this reading depoliticizes the family and the process of migration. Morris's critique is important to this book's continuation of this project to understand immigrant family dynamics in their political contexts.

The complexities of the relationship between generations are not strictly familial matters. Some generational readings of immigrant families (both sociological and fictional) make the mistake of accepting the idea of the private sphere, in which the conflicts of immigrant families are nonpolitical and solely cultural, based on a self-evident "culture clash" between the "traditional" home culture and the "modernity" of the site of settlement. In the Asian American context, Lisa Lowe rejects the "master narratives of generational conflict and filial relation" as the primary means of interpreting Asian American culture because they essentialize and homogenize Asian American people and "privatize social struggles" (135). Lowe's critique of this approach to the immigrant family is insightful and important, but rather than take it as an endorsement of throwing out a generational model altogether, I see her argument as pointing out the need to repoliticize readings of generational divides, highlighting the complex ways that they interact with the material struggles, political contexts, and societal pressures that surround and constitute them. This is especially relevant in the context of Black immigrants because of the centrality of race and anti-Black racism to the political and social structure of US society.

Much scholarship exploring intergenerational relationships within immigrant families in the US is written about Asian American contexts. Indeed, part of the impetus behind my project is to expand on the relatively small amount of critical writing that explores equally the immigrant and Black nature of Black immigrant literature by drawing on both theories focused on gender and migration as well as theories focused on gender and Blackness. Perhaps because Blackness in America is strongly tied to the forced migration of the transatlantic slave trade, the seemingly voluntary nature of economic migration that characterizes the arrival of many African and Caribbean immigrants has been difficult to explore in relation to their involuntary induction into the American racial hierarchy. Recognizing similarity does not have to mean losing sight of difference and vice versa; applying Asian American theories to Caribbean American and continental African American contexts can be elucidating without flattening out the significant differences between Asian and Black racialization in the US.

Exploring how narratives of immigration and narratives of Blackness are constructed in the United States requires understanding the ways that these discourses are constructed in relation to many of the same basic assumptions but manifest in different ways. Both narratives start with the assertion of white, European-descended ownership of the Americas by right of conquest, from which follows the belief that belonging is based on the ability to merge with this population.[5] Laws governing the lives of African Americans, from the very beginning of US settlement to the present day, were established to prevent any such merger. African Americans are therefore recognized as always present but never fundamentally a part of the nation.[6] Immigrants are seen as either capable or incapable of achieving this merger based on a number of factors, as was seen in relation to Irish, Italian, and Jewish immigrants, among others, whose transformation from aliens to (often) indistinguishable members of the white America that remains the center of American identity

---

5. This premise also governs the exclusion of Native Americans from the nation as well, though in ways that are different from both African Americans and immigrants.

6. Michelle M. Wright demonstrates this dynamic when she discusses Thomas Jefferson's *Notes on the State of Virginia*, in which he "posits the 'Negro' as a malevolent force that may physically reside within the nation yet remains psychically Other to that nation, not unlike a nasty virus on the national body whose sole aim, as dictated by nature, is to weaken and ultimately destroy that nation" (8).

has been well documented and explored. The "perpetual foreigner" status of those immigrant groups not admitted into whiteness exists in a strange middle ground between the African American position, which is also in many ways a perpetual foreigner position, and the white hegemony that offers immigrants the promise of eventual acceptance based on the premise that they are being benevolently allowed to enter into the nation and find a place for themselves within it. In other words, the opportunity for merging is promised even if it is rarely fulfilled.

Asian American scholars have done a great deal of work exploring the contours of the perpetual foreigner position as it relates to immigrants and, importantly, as it has been mobilized to create the idea of the model minority which has been used to both punish African Americans and keep Asian Americans in line. The concept of the model minority has been applied to Afro-Caribbean immigrants as early as the 1960s (Ifatunji 112) and African immigrants in more recent years (Ukpokodu 70). Black conservatives like Thomas Sowell have long used Caribbean immigrants to produce a "cultural" argument for poverty experienced by African Americans by arguing that what economically differentiates Caribbean immigrants from their African American counterparts are their positive cultural traits like thrift and hard work (James 224). This is, of course, a classic use of model-minority discourse. Evidence that the model-minority classification of African immigrants has gone mainstream is that Amy Chua, the best-selling author of the controversial *Battle Hymn of the Tiger Mother*, includes Nigerians in her list of "successful groups in American society" alongside Chinese, Jewish, Indian, Iranian, and Lebanese people as well as Cuban exiles and Mormons in her follow-up, *The Triple Package: How Three Unlikely Traits Explain the Rise and Fall of Cultural Groups in America*. However unevenly, African and Caribbean immigrants have been incorporated into the model-minority category. As such, the case of African and Caribbean immigrants offers in turn insight into the nature and complexity of the idea of the model minority that can help to develop a deeper understanding of and a greater ability to resist this positioning.

The term *model minority* was popularized in 1966 through the publication of an article in *U.S. News & World Report*, although the basis of the idea dates back to the nineteenth century (Nguyen 146). The consensus among Asian American scholars is that the model minority refers to how

> the structure of domination that favors whites and is controlled by them positions Asian Americans as a minority that can succeed without government or social assistance, through sheer hard work and perseverance based

upon a system of social values that prioritizes family, education, and sacrifice. These social values that all Asian Americans reputedly share, often referred to as Confucian, accurately or otherwise, also prioritize obedience and hierarchy, which means that Asian Americans are reluctant to blame others for any lack in their social position and are willing to accept their social position with gratitude. Asian Americans are therefore a model minority because they demonstrate to other minorities what can be achieved through self-reliance rather than government assistance, self-sacrifice rather than self-interest, and quiet restraint rather than vocal complaint in the face of perceived or actual injustice. (Nguyen 146–47)

These values are supposed by American hegemonic discourse to be the reason that Asian Americans "succeed" more than African Americans, as opposed to less palatable reasons such as differential treatment based on race or the long history of economic deprivation and racial terror visited upon African Americans.

The ideological use of the model-minority idea for American hegemony is clear, but erin Khuê Ninh warns against the common ways that Asian American scholars engage with it. She argues that while "a central tenet of the model minority *thesis* [is] that the model minority identity is a *myth*," the model minority has become an internalized and actively pursued identity within the Asian immigrant family: "The heart of the issue is not whether an Asian immigrant family currently meets the socioeconomic or professional measures of the model minority. Rather, the issue is whether it aspires to do so, whether it *applies* those metrics" (9). Ninh argues that "an identity's materiality is perhaps more appropriately gauged by its fictions and active identifications (what its discourses aim to fabricate) than merely by its present circumstances" (9). Thus, for Ninh and for me, what makes the model minority real is not whether immigrants and their children are successful or compliant but rather whether they aim to be. Because most Asian Americans (and, as this book explores, most Caribbean and continental African Americans) are "post-1965 arrivals" or their children, they

> have been intravenously injected into the climate of material access . . . in the immediate wake and ongoing mobilization of model minority discourse. If they recognize U.S. racism not in the lineage of social movement coalitions, but rather in terms of the glass ceiling, this is but in keeping with their parents' (neoconservative) convictions and training: that their children must excel to overcompensate for disadvantage in the racial hierarchy. (Ninh 10)

This "glass ceiling" way of understanding US racism does not pretend that it does not exist but fails to see its complexity or its less overt versions. This focus especially on career success and economic security discourages considering other metrics of happiness or belonging that are less capitalist in orientation. Thus, for Ninh, if scholars mean to seriously engage contemporary Asian American culture and politics, they need to reckon with the reality that "the assimilationist, individualist, upwardly mobile professional class of the model minority is, for familial intents and purposes, Asian America's model children," and, as such, "an effective understanding of the Asian American subject's relation to the nation must therefore come to terms with the immigrant family as that nation's intermediary and agent" (Ninh 11). Ninh further argues that the Asian American immigrant family is a particular "production unit" that aims to produce good capitalist subjects (2); a core aspect of what makes it the model minority is that it works within the capitalist imperative of US American society. The internalization of model-minority ideas and their imposition within the family and the wider community is just as present in the novels of Black immigrant women writers as those of their Asian immigrant counterparts. In this project, by making a connection between the politics of respectability laid out above and the ways that an iteration of the model-minority idea *is applied to and internalized by* Black immigrants, I demonstrate how these two discourses create the condition in which the daughterly subjects I analyze grow up and rebel.

In order to ground this project in scholarship that prioritizes the intersection of race, gender, and migration, I read Susan Morris and erin Khuê Ninh's work alongside each other in order to build a framework for addressing the particularities of immigrant and second-generation Black girls' positionality. Through this bringing together, I map how immigrant Black girls find themselves at the intersection of respectability politics and model-minority discourse. These discourses are themselves actually mirrors of each other despite their seemingly different applications.

This book asserts the possibility of coalition-building that is responsive to both sameness and difference, often simultaneously. Morris is a particularly ideal critic to contribute to the framework of this project, as she is herself the daughter of Caribbean immigrants to the US, and this subject position shapes her vision. She writes, "As someone who was born in the Caribbean and was raised in Caribbean immigrant communities in the United States, I certainly see the differences between experiences of Blacks in the Caribbean and the United States, but I do not find Caribbean and U.S. Black identities to be necessarily mutually exclusive" (13). My analysis of immigrant and second-generation Blackness in the US is based on the recognition of both these differences and this lack of mutual exclusivity. I also aim to "resist collapsing or conflating Black women's experiences across regions" (Morris 14), by tracing the tension between those experiences when placed into the same region. In so doing, I demonstrate that Black immigrant and second-generation women writers are attentive to Avtar Brah's important assertion about the value of a politics of identification as opposed to a politics of identity:

> The constitution of subjectivity within heterogeneous discursive practices means that we inhabit articulating and changing identities interweaving across relations of race, gender, class or sexuality. How we work with and across our "differences" would depend upon the political and conceptual frameworks which inform our understanding of these "differences." It is our political perspectives and commitments that determine the basis for effective coalition building. I believe that coalitions are possible through a politics of identification, as opposed to a "politics of identity." (93)

Black immigrant women writers can identify the ways that their characters both are and are not a part of African America and use both these similarities and differences to fuel their coalition-building with African Americans.

In this book, I argue Black immigrant women's fiction rejects the depoliticization of the family and instead recognizes the home space as a site where multiple competing discourses shape the lives of immigrant and second-generation Black girls. In other words, this work hopes to repoliticize readings of the Black immigrant family in a way that is responsive to the particularities of their immigranthood. erin Khuê Ninh's monograph *Ingratitude: The Debt-Bound Daughter in Asian American Literature* provides a thoughtful model for such repoliticization. Ninh's work is also a model for this project's multiethnic and decade-spanning scope in that she argues for the necessity of looking at the ways that textual themes and conflicts cross a multitude of differences; she points out that "the intergenerational conflict—its forms of power, its discourses of subject formation—replicates with compelling faithfulness across an era of seemingly imposing historical change" (3). The value of identifying and examining such consistencies across difference is at the very heart of this project.

The combination of the model minority and intergenerational conflict produces several results that Ninh identifies and that I apply to the African and Caribbean contexts explored in this book. The most prominent of these structures is "designated failure," which she describes as "a key stone of familial discourse." She continues, "the construct of 'filial obligation' defines the parent-child relation as a debtor-creditor relation, but within the system without contract or consent, the parent-creditor brings into being a child-debtor who can never repay the debt of her own inception and rearing" (16). This debtor-creditor relationship defies the idea that the daughter's life can be her own; how can she come of age and go out into the world if her life is just an extension of her parents' lives because of her unending obligation to fulfill a debt that she never willfully incurred?

Ninh applies her challenging and compelling argument about the immigrant family structure specifically to the work of Asian North American women writers. She asserts that while immigrant families do not uniformly apply the systems she identifies, "if the question is whether these daughterly narratives equally know the model minority and model filiality as a common paradigm, then—incredibly across ethnicity, class, religion, and immigration decade—I believe the answer would have to be yes" (162). I take her argument further by identifying the consistent presence of the debt-bound daughter and the political economy of the immigrant home in American texts about other immigrant communities, particularly Black immigrant communities.

The relevance of Ninh's argument in relation to Black immigrant communities is most visible when considering the gendered nature of how model-minority discourse and model filiality are applied. I explore one particularly prevalent element of this gendered context throughout this book: the way that controlling daughters' sexuality appears consistently as a preoccupation in the family structures represented by Black immigrant women writers. Ninh raises the questions, "*What is invested in female virginity* such that a family should insist upon keeping its reputation between its daughters' legs, and what purpose would such an ill-advised arrangement serve?" (128). The centrality of controlling girls' bodies to immigrant family structures is, as Ninh points out, strange and self-defeating, yet it is also relentlessly consistent. Like Ninh, I will not be exploring the origin of this system, because that goes beyond what reading literature can offer, but I will be examining what purpose it serves in the present of each text to see how these writers make sense of this ongoing system of control.

In many ways, Susana Morris's work examines the mothers against whom the rebellious daughters I discuss are rebelling. She highlights the ways that Black women writers demonstrate the dangers of conformity, while this project highlights the way that they use rebellion to explore the complexities of resisting the paradox of respectability. She writes that "Black women's writing also depicts the strains of family relationships beneath the façade of stability and respectability. Novels frequently portray female characters who question or struggle with adherence to the ideals of respectability politics, yet persist in policing others' behavior under the same rubric" (9). As my analysis will demonstrate, the mothers in these novels frequently enact this seeming hypocrisy. Their struggles with respectability do not stop them from enforcing it onto their daughters, whose rebellion against it is often made more complex because of the rebellious daughter's recognition of her mother's own struggle.

These mothers are portrayed as existing in a space of ambivalence. Morris writes, "Black women writers configure ambivalence in a variety of ways, perhaps most notably through portrayals of familial relationships marked by intense notions of duty, honor, and respect coupled with thinly veiled enmity, indifference, estrangement, repression, and even outright domination and/or violence" (9–10). This potent and potentially poisonous combination of impulses displayed by their mothers places daughters in a dangerous position. Ninh makes the astute point that

> while there is no question that the losses of immigration matter, that institutional racism and media representation figure into the second-generation experience, so too does power in the most intimate, vulnerable, and formative social contexts—one which may demand that the subject compensate for familial losses by successfully navigating hostile social and political waters, and which may very well redouble the stakes of "racial" failure. (5)

The site of the family as a refuge from the hostilities of, or even the experience of invisibility in, the outside world makes the familial home all the more complex and dangerous when it is also a site of rejection, excessive discipline, or even trauma. Just because authority is not malicious does not mean that it is incapable of doing harm (Ninh 8). The ambivalence that Morris identifies is one of the core objects of rebellion that this project explores.

The role of mothers in constraining the sexuality of daughters may often be framed as serving a purpose related to men—saving the daughter for her future husband, protecting the reputation of the father, etc.—but the active use of this particular mode of control is often more complex than this seemingly outward-facing reasoning. The emphasis on mother-daughter relationships in Black immigrant texts highlights that it is important not to "take gendering authority to be synonymous with patriarchy or the patriarch alone" (Ninh 129). Morris stresses the same nuance by using the term *kyriarchy* as opposed to *patriarchy* (9). By exploring women's investment in the kind of social and sexual control both Morris and Ninh describe, I complicate the sometimes simplistic readings of the gender relationships in Black immigrant fiction, which can at times be used to cast Black fathers (or their absence) as the antagonist of these stories.

Literary Analysis as Feminist Praxis

This project is also rooted in the history of feminist analysis that rejects the idea of Western superiority. In her seminal essay "Under Western Eyes," Chandra Talpade Mohanty critiques the way that Western feminism produces discourses of Third World difference that "are predicated upon (and hence obviously bring into sharper focus) assumptions about Western women as secular, liberated, and having control over their own lives" (353). In other words, Western feminists at times use the supposed subjugation of their Others to bolster their own sense of freedom. This discourse holds true not just toward the Third World women who live elsewhere; it has also frequently been applied to immigrant and second-generation women living in the West, who are seen as needing to be liberated from the chains of their ancestral culture. Mainstream social discourses of assimilation are therefore mixed with feminist ideas about women's liberation to cast immigrant and second-generation women as victims of their ethnic or religious identities, whose emancipation from patriarchal power is coextensive with their adaptation to Western values, lifestyles, and identity categories. Of course, as Mohanty points out in the context of writing about the Third World, this "West is best" attitude homogenizes and objectifies women whose lived realities are significantly more complex and nuanced. Moreover, this attitude obscures the patriarchal structures, practices, and ideologies still very much present within Western societies, especially those that intersect significantly with racial hierarchies and stereotypes. After all, as many feminists have pointed out from the beginning of the movement (see, for example, hooks's *From Margin to Center*), the liberation available to middle-class white women differs significantly from what is afforded to Black women and women of color more broadly, as well as poor women of any race, and is indeed at times achieved on their backs.[7] Since many if not most immigrants are playing economic catch-up upon arrival in the site of settlement, racial and wealth disparities impact their lives directly.

I am not arguing that there are not patriarchal familial dynamics in Black immigrant families, just as Mohanty is not arguing that there is no sexism or gender discrimination in the Third World. Rather, the nature of such dynamics needs to be more specifically and thoughtfully explored. Instead, I want to examine how the patriarchy within the family home and the patriarchy in the

---

7. Indeed, a parallel might be drawn here between the liberation of middle-class white women on the backs of women of color and poor women and the greater equality achieved by African Americans through participation in the US's imperial ventures overseas, which Boyce Davies explores through an examination of Audre Lorde's poem "Equal Opportunity" (Boyce Davies 26).

wider society present dual pressures that the female characters in the texts I explore find themselves caught between. They must navigate both, not just reject one for the other. Neither the familial home nor the wider society are wholly liberatory nor wholly oppressive.

All of the complexities and contradictions described above should make it obvious that this project must be grounded in a transversal politics. This term was coined by Italian feminists and expanded upon by a variety of other feminist writers, including Patricia Hill Collins, whose writing on the subject is particularly influential in this work. Hill Collins points out that "transversal politics requires a basic rethinking of cognitive frameworks used to understand the world and to change it. Transversal politics requires rejecting the binary thinking that has been so central to oppressions of race, class, gender, sexuality, and nation" and goes on to describe how this binary thinking limits our ability to think intersectionally because it depends on seeing single events or situations as having single causes and seeing people as either one thing or another, "a racist or an antiracist individual, a sexist person or not, an oppressor group or oppressed one" (265). Such thinking cannot meaningfully address the lived experience of Black women, or anyone else for that matter. Transversal politics, instead, "requires both/and thinking. In such frameworks, all individuals and groups possess varying amounts of penalty and privilege in one historically created system" (265). This perspective allows for politics that are responsive to multiple axes of both penalty and privilege and how they can be operating simultaneously. A daughter of well-off, professional Ghanaian migrants can have class and economic privilege while being penalized for her race in predominantly white contexts, yet she may also gain privilege in contrast to an African American peer in those same contexts by virtue of her immigrant identity, even as in her own life she may recall instances during which she was bullied by African American peers for reasons based on ingrained anti-African sentiment among Americans.

An example such as the one above demonstrates Hill Collins's point that "depending on context, individuals and groups may be alternately oppressors in some settings, oppressed in others, or simultaneously oppressing and oppressed in still others" (265). Bringing this more nuanced approach to understanding the systems in which we live allows us to recognize that "group histories are relational" (Hill Collins 266). African and Caribbean immigrant communities within the US have complex relationships with all of the other parts of that system, including but by no means limited to African American communities, other immigrant communities, and the white mainstream with all of its own complexities of class, region, and status. In the novels that this book explores, the Black female protagonists seek to navigate these relationships, and their experiences reveal the necessity of approaching them with an actively transversal politics, either through doing so themselves or by not doing so and suffering because of it.

US Black feminism undoubtedly informs this project even as I mark the notable absence of Black immigrant women in the conceptualization of US Black feminism.[8] In her seminal work *Black Feminist Thought*, Hill Collins acknowledges the diversity of class positions among African American women and notes that "varying ethnic and citizenship statuses within the U.S. nation-state as well also shape differences among Black women in the United States" (32). Yet the example she uses for this is Black Puerto Ricans, who—while as she rightly notes, "hold[ ] a special form of American citizenship" (32)—are not technically immigrants (however uncomfortable their place within the nation-state). She goes on to recognize US Black women as members of the wider African diaspora and asserts that "Black diasporic frameworks center analyses of Black women within the context of common challenges experienced transnationally" (32). She concludes this section by arguing that "placing African-American women's experiences, thought, and practice in a transnational, Black diasporic context reveals these and other commonalities of women of African descent while specifying what is particular to African-American women" (33). In effect, Hill Collins identifies the diversity among African American women and the interconnectedness of Black women globally, but she does not fully manage to connect the two through a recognition of immigrant Black women living within the US. *African American* (which she explicitly ties to a distinctive history of "forced immigration to the United States and subsequent enslavement" [Hill Collins 32]) and *Black* within the US context remain synonymous even as she notes diasporic connections, demonstrating the strangely invisible place of immigrant Black women within African American discourses. This is not a criticism of Hill Collins; the question of what to do with these diasporic interconnections when they converge on American soil is complex and not her focus. Rather, I see this exclusion as a symptom of the ambivalent positioning of Black immigrant women, who are not "over there" subjects of US Black women's transnational solidarity but are also seen as holding an "irregular" form of Blackness. Hill Collins, when discussing the "differential consideration" of diverse US Black women, notes that "not every *individual* Black woman consumer need experience being followed in a store as a potential shoplifter, ignored while others are waited on first, or

---

8. This has been the topic of numerous panels at the National Women's Studies Association (NWSA) conference over the years and was indeed a key aspect of the theme of the 2020 conference, "The Poetics, Politics and Praxis of Transnational Feminisms," unfortunately canceled because of the COVID-19 pandemic.

seated near restaurant kitchens and rest rooms, for African-American women as a collectivity to recognize that differential *group* treatment is operating" (29). Importantly, immigrant Black women are also subject to this same differential group treatment regardless of whether or not they are perceived as part of the group.

Immigrant Black women's ambivalent position is particularly clear in discussions of the transnational because of the way that their individual transnational positionality complicates ideas about transnational solidarity that presuppose physical distance. In the same work, Hill Collins advocates for the situating of US Black feminism in a transnational context that recognizes the overlapping concerns of women of African descent all over the world. She asserts that

> Black women in Nigeria, Trinidad and Tobago, the United Kingdom, Botswana, Brazil, and other nation-states are similarly located. They encounter the contours of local social movements, the policies of their nation-states, and the same global matrix of domination in which U.S. Black women are situated. All these groups of women thus are positioned with situations of domination that are characterized by intersecting oppressions, yet their angle of vision on domination vary greatly. (250)

Hill Collins is working to establish a sense of African diasporic solidarity among women of African descent while avoiding providing a homogenous view of this large, dispersed, and diverse group. She acknowledges that "developing this Black diasporic perspective among African-American women can be more difficult than one thinks, especially given the limited contact with Black women from the United Kingdom, Senegal, Brazil, and other nation-states, as well as the historically insular view of the world that permeates U.S. society" (255). Her diagnosis of US insularity is very much correct, but the idea that there is limited contact between African American women and Black women from elsewhere once again overlooks the presence of those women from elsewhere within the United States.

Demographic data like the information I presented earlier in this introduction is one way to point out that there is more contact than one might imagine. Another way to demonstrate the ways that non-American Black women have consistently found themselves playing a role in African American community and discourse is through recognizing the presence of culturally important figures as diverse as June Jordan, Audre Lorde, Malcolm X, Grace Jones, Foxy Brown, and the Notorious B.I.G., all born to Caribbean immigrant mothers. The presence of immigrant Black women within the United States produces an up-close-and-personal opportunity to examine how "placing U.S. Black women's experiences in a transnational context shifts [the Black/White binary] understanding of U.S. Black feminism. Instead of being White feminism in black-face, the core themes of U.S. Black feminism resemble similar issues raised by women of African descent elsewhere" (Hill Collins 252). Black immigrant women represent both the "here" and the "elsewhere" of US Black feminism.

Subject Formation

Another core element of this project's approach to rebellious Black immigrant daughters is the exploration of the relationship between coming-of-age and subject formation. Since this project is fundamentally interested in racialization and gender construction, it must contend with how these processes are conceptualized and depicted. I see these processed as central aspects of subject formation. As such, I explore how Black immigrant coming-of-age narratives use the process of coming-of-age to represent the closely related but not identical process of subject formation. In his work on coming-of-age narratives in American literature, Kenneth Millard notes that

> the contemporary novel of adolescence is often characterised by a concerted attempt to situate the protagonist in relation to historical contexts or points of origin by which individuals come to understand themselves as having been conditioned. The individual novel often reveals a temporal structure in which the contemporary moment of coming-of-age is contextualised gradually by a consciousness of historical events that are antecedent to it and deeply inform it. (10)

Narratives of coming-of-age are invested in understanding the self as historically and socially situated, and as such, coming-of-age is intrinsically tied to subject formation.

Subject formation refers to the idea that a person is both a subject in the sense of a being who experiences the world subjectively as well as a being who is subject to the world around them. Individuals are acted upon by power. Power does not just subordinate; it forms them into subjects, and, as Judith Butler writes, "provid[es] the very condition of [their] existence and the trajectory of [their] desire" (2). Both coming-of-age and subject formation are processes of becoming. While subject formation can be considered a lifelong experience, it is particularly visible in childhood. Butler again notes that "a child's love is prior to judgement and decision; a child tended and nourished in a 'good enough' way will love, and only later stand a chance of discriminating among those he or she loves" (8) and connects this point to the idea that "there is no possibility of not loving, where love is bound up with the requirements of life. The child does not know to what he/she attaches; yet the infant as well as the child must attach in order to persist in and as itself" (8). For Butler, this is an example of the nature of subjection, whereby "a subject is not only formed in subordination, but that this subordination provides the subject's continuing condition of possibility" (8). Children are literally the subjects of their parents, and this relationship reflects their position as subjects in the wider social world. The processes of subjection that take place in childhood are not separable from the other elements of identity formation that we tend to associate with coming-of-age, because they are mutually informing; the desire for individuation so central to discourses of coming-of-age is simultaneous with the sense that "the desire to persist in one's own being requires submitting to a world of others that is fundamentally not one's own (a submission that does not take place at a later date, but which frames and makes possible the desire to be)" (Butler 28). The combination of these two interconnected yet distinct processes, subject formation and coming-of-age, in literature suggests that portraying what is traditionally thought of as the transition from innocence to experience is an attractive means to make intelligible the complex process of subject formation, which draws attention to the social construction of identity. That is to say, such texts use the depiction of the seemingly universal and natural process of growing up to explore how the social, political, and discursive context into which the child emerges is what creates the "self" of the child, who is a subject in the Foucauldian sense.

Contrary to a vision of coming-of-age wherein the process results in an autonomous and internally coherent individual, the coming-of-age narratives I study instead produce an image of their protagonists that makes visible the forces of power that turn them into subjects. The "modes of objectification which transform human beings into subjects," particularly what Foucault terms "dividing practices" by which "the subject is either divided inside himself or divided from others" (208), are foregrounded. In conceptualizing subject formation in the context of coming-of-age, I draw on Avtar Brah's point that "identity may be understood as that very process by which the multiplicity, contradiction, and instability of subjectivity is signified as having coherence, continuity, stability; as having a core—a continually changing core but the sense of a core nonetheless—that at any given moment is enunciated as the 'I'" (123). The process of coming-of-age is the process of creating this sense of a core; it is the articulation of the "I" out of the complexities of subjectivity, not as a denial of these complexities but as willful acts of amalgamation.

Furthermore, my focus on Black immigrant and second-generation girls connects subject formation with processes of racialization. In these texts, becoming subjects means becoming imbued with a racial identity that is produced both internally and externally. The characters' coming-of-age is inextricably linked to subject formation that is simultaneous with the development of a form of racial identification. I also foreground the way that gender identities are constructed through these processes, emphasizing the intersectionality of racialization and gender construction. As has been highlighted by numerous scholars, migration itself is a highly gendered experience. For the daughter of immigrants, the gender dynamics of the ancestral homeland and of the site of settlement produce a new set of dynamics shaped by the realities of immigrant family life so that her process of gender construction is neither like that of her mother nor of her nondiasporic peers. It is important not to think of each of these processes as sitting on top of each other like differently flavored layers of a cake, touching yet separate, but rather as all present in the batter. I refer to the set of processes that I have just described as *coming into being as coming into difference*.

Texts that focus on the children of immigrants, and by extension, the effects of migration, necessarily grapple with the theme of growing into difference from previous ways of being, because the fact of migration creates a literal and figurative departure. This departure is compounded by the simultaneous difference that is a result of arrival. Through depictions of coming-of-age, second-generation-focused texts explore how *coming into being as coming into difference* is a multidirectional experience. This multidirectionality means that the common model of understanding coming-of-age narratives that assumes a singular society that the protagonist must conform to, or reject, is a false construction. This multidirectionality is a key element of immigrant and second-generation narratives of coming-of-age. These texts often highlight the plurality of societies with which their characters engage. As children of migrants, these subjects must define themselves in relation to ancestral homeland(s), the mainstream societies of sites of settlement, the unique communities formed by immigrants in sites of settlement, and the other minoritized communities that they may encounter. If coming-of-age is largely about developing a functional relationship with society, what happens when one must do so in relation to multiple societies? And if these multiple societies have different or overlapping forms of social expectations and structures, some of which are deeply oppressive and which are often deeply gendered and raced, how does one navigate them all at once? This multidirectionality produces the "migratory subjectivity" that Boyce Davies argues means that "the subject is not just constituted, but in being constituted has multiple identities that do not always make for harmony" (36). The conditions produced by the immigrant family's internalization of respectability politics and model-minority discourse offer a prime example of this multidirectionality.

Form

The novels that I explore in the coming chapters take on these complex questions and more as they present immigrant and second-generation Black girls whose positioning within their families, communities, nations, and relationships force them into states of covert and overt rebellion. The nature and form of their rebellions vary widely, as do their motivations and their end results. What they all share is a deeply intersectional approach to their characters' experiences.

Flowing chronologically, each chapter of this book works together to build a complex picture of the figure of the rebellious Black immigrant or second-generation daughter. The first chapter, "Rebelling in the In-Between" takes up Paule Marshall's 1959 novel *Brown Girl, Brownstones* as one of the earliest examples of Afro-Caribbean second-generation writing in the US that explores the key themes of this book. This chapter examines Marshall's representation of the Barbadian community in New York City during and after World War II. In it, I argue that the protagonist is a rebellious daughter who is keenly aware of the gendered expectations of behavior foisted upon her within her immigrant home and becomes cognizant of the powerful yet nebulous forces of racism in US society. The coming together of these two forces in her life demonstrates the ways in which Black women and girls are constrained by the enforcement of respectability politics and model-minority discourse. Central to the novel's exploration of these conditions is the contrast between the protagonist's mother and father, as they demonstrate the multiple and deeply gendered strategies of assimilation or withdrawal practiced by the first generation. The first generation is contrasted with the US-born second generation, who, despite the first generation's desire to dictate their behavior and identity, have different racial sensibilities and coping strategies of their own.

In chapter 2, "Rebelling against Repetition," I focus on Edwidge Danticat's 1994 novel *Breath, Eyes, Memory*, which tells the story of a young girl born in Haiti and then brought to live with her mother in New York City in the 1980s, who must navigate both her mother's experience of trauma that led to her birth and the trauma inflicted upon her by her mother. While Haitian immigrants are rarely perceived through the lens of the model minority, this novel makes clear that the expectations of respectability and the immigrant desire for social mobility are nevertheless present and powerful within that community. I argue that this novel reveals the importance of enacting a nuanced reading of rebellion, as the protagonist's most overt rebellion serves to reproduce the traumas of the past while her more subtle form of rebellion against the rules of respectability—speaking what is usually kept silent—is what creates the possibility of a better future. This chapter's exploration of Danticat's novel expands on the theme of intergenerational conflict present in chapter 1 by demonstrating how many of the same tensions between immigrant Black and African American identity persist throughout the course of the twentieth century.

In the second half of this book, I shift my focus from Caribbean immigrant texts to those written by and about continental Africans. The third chapter, "Self-Destructive Rebellion," engages with Taiye Selasi's 2013 novel *Ghana Must Go*, which explores the reconnection of the Ghanaian American Sai family following the death of their estranged patriarch. Unlike the first two novels addressed in this book, *Ghana Must Go* offers not just one coming-of-age narrative but several, through the depiction of the four Sai children, two girls and two boys. Focusing on the Sai daughters, I argue that this novel carries out the most nuanced exploration of the tension between the model-minority characterization of African immigrants and the experience of American racialization for the second generation through its depiction of how the immigrant desire to silence the colonial and difficult past as a way of protecting and freeing their children is potentially well-meaning but ultimately disastrous and even, in the end, cowardly. In analyzing the different and at times self-destructive nature of the daughters' rebellions, I also argue that the silencing of the past leads to the misdirection of rebellious instincts against the self rather than in a more empowering direction.

The fourth chapter, "Rebelling against Stereotypes and Confinement," analyzes Chimamanda Ngozi Adichie's 2013 novel *Americanah* to consider how the racial and gendered dynamics at the heart of this project differ when the protagonist immigrates while still in the process of coming-of-age. Adichie's novel follows a young Nigerian woman through her youth in Nigeria into her migration to the US as a university student and beyond. This chapter argues that Adichie's active engagement with the gender-inflected racialization of Black immigrants through the protagonist's blog makes explicit the dynamics that served as powerful undercurrents in the previously explored novels. At the same time, this novel chooses the uncommon route of having the protagonist give up on living in America altogether, a direction made possible by a specific set of national and economic circumstances in Nigeria in the early twenty-first century as well as the protagonist's Nigerian upbringing, which sets her apart from her second-generation American counterparts.

"Against" signals both closeness and separation, intimacy and rejection. For the daughters of immigrants, what does it mean to both love and rebel against the family? To both identify with the nation and feel a sense of unbelonging within it? How might they resist patriarchal and oppressive norms within the family and within the site of settlement and find a sense of their own agency, their own imagination, and their own identity? The texts that I study reflect on these questions, sometimes providing tentative answers and sometimes asking even more questions in return. By recognizing how the Black immigrant girls who populate the novels I am exploring experience this againstness as both necessary and stifling, I see their writers as embracing the space of being against as a fruitful site of growth and of knowledge. As readers, we can enter into that space of *against* and consider the different visions of family, nation, and identity that emerge from submitting to this place of discomfort. Narratives of rebellion that are not prescriptive but rather demand a recognition of why the need for rebellion emerges and the complexity of what it might look like lay bare the many ways that discomfort demands ingenuity and imagination.

CHAPTER 1

Rebelling in the In-Between

The figure of the rebellious daughter is often in conflict with the same thing—parental control—but enacts her rebellion in distinct and sometimes surprising ways. Indeed, this rebellion is rarely singular, and different approaches to rebellion can yield wildly varied results. In this chapter, I read one of the earliest novels to represent a Black immigrant community in the United States in order to explore a rebellious daughter of immigrants who is at once archetypical, setting the stage for many daughters to come, and deeply individual, approaching her rebellion in a way that is deeply rooted in social and familial circumstances that are strongly tied to the first half of the twentieth century and the specific location of Brooklyn.

Paule Marshall's 1959 novel *Brown Girl, Brownstones* follows Selina, a young New York–born daughter of Bajan immigrants. The family, made up of Selina, her mother, her father, and her withdrawn sister, rents an old, formerly opulent brownstone divided into separate apartments. Selina's mother, Silla, longs to buy the building, while her frequently unemployed husband, Deighton, is uninterested in pursuing this goal. When Deighton inherits a piece of land in Barbados, Silla urges him to sell it so that they can afford to buy the brownstone. Deighton refuses, dreaming of returning home to Barbados and building a home there. Through subterfuge, Silla is able to sell the land, but rather than using the money to buy the brownstone, Deighton squanders it. This cements the rift between the two parents, ultimately leading to Deighton's religious conversion, deportation, and death. Several years later, as Selina is reaching maturity, she must come to terms with her parents' past to chart her own future. While Selina's parents play a significant role in the novel, the conflict at the center of it is not the one actively taking place between the parents so much as the ongoing conflict within Selina that the contrast between her parents makes visible.

As Selina comes of age, she grapples with her racialization, gender construction, and personal identity in a way that is shaped by her parents' distinct characters and belief systems. In her father, Selina sees the false yet alluring promise of masculinity, while with her mother she cringes away from the stark reality of what womanhood has to offer. The consistent description of her mother as "the mother" suggests both a universality to her mother's impossible position as well as Selina's desire to distance herself from the woman who she loves, hates, and fears becoming. At the same time, she finds herself thrust into American racial dynamics and unsure how to navigate the ways her Blackness and her Bajan ancestry affect her life. Ultimately, I argue that Marshall's exploration of the Barbadian immigrant community in World War II–era New York City through the eyes of a rebellious daughter reveals how the intense confluence of gendered expectations of behavior within the immigrant home and the powerful and amorphous forms of racism in US society suffocates the expression and mobility of Black immigrant women and girls. In particular, the central conflict between the protagonist's mother and father makes visible the diverse and highly gendered ways in which the first generation navigates—or fails to navigate—the pressures of their positionality, and how that generation projects their strategies onto the second generation, whose experiences as US-born children shape their sensibilities in ways that diverge significantly from those of their parents.

In some ways, the familial dynamic in Marshall's novel is the most normative of all of the families explored in this book. Silla's capitalist approach to upward mobility, Selina's artistic ambitions, and Deighton's ineffectual grasping for masculinity fit an archetype of immigrant experience that has solidified over the last century. What sets *Brown Girl, Brownstones* apart is that its modernist style breathes a psychological complexity into these positions that demand readers acknowledge that each immigrant family that is shaped and, in this case, torn asunder by the forces of capitalism, racism, patriarchy, and the expectations that they produce is made up of people whose subjectivity is unique even if their situation is not. As Barbara Christian points out in her oft-cited chapter on the novels of Paule Marshall, an important aspect of Marshall's writing is "her sculpting of women characters who at first glance might seem to be the stereotypical contours of the black woman. Under her careful, tender, yet incisive hands, these outlines are transformed into distinct women. She shows us that if we glance too quickly, we might see only the outline of the domineering mother, the black prostitute, the martyred mother" (80). Marshall demands of her readers a concentrated gaze. Despite the novel being focused on Selina's subjectivity, the narrative paints a psychologically rich picture of Silla and Deighton, demonstrating the second-generation desire to understand the immigrant generation even while critiquing it. The novel's attention to racialization and the way that the perception of Black immigrant communities differed from both other migrants who came before and African Americans demonstrates how important it is to situate any reading of this novel in both a diasporic and an American context.

Scholarly engagement with *Brown Girl, Brownstones* has been significant, although it has decreased in recent years. Barbara Christian's analysis, which I have already mentioned, provides an in-depth close reading of the novel, with a particular emphasis on the psychological makeup of Silla and Deighton. Later studies of the novel focus on the problem and potential of ethnic community (Japtok; Cobb); mother-daughter relationships, both blood and otherwise (Troester); and the novel's treatment of sexuality (King). All of these elements of the novel are relevant to this analysis of Selina's trajectory as a rebellious daughter, and this chapter aims to probe more explicitly the intersections of community, family, and society as they act upon the individual character. I also include analysis of Marshall's novel in this volume to bring it into critical conversation with works published after the scholarly attention to *Brown Girl, Brownstones* dropped off, in order to reestablish its foundational role in second-generation representation.

The novel's opening, through its description of a row of brownstones, introduces its theme of sameness and difference existing simultaneously. On the one hand, "glancing down the interminable Brooklyn street you thought of those joined brownstones as one house reflected through a train of mirrors, with no walls between the houses but only vast rooms yawning endlessly one into another" (1). Yet this uniformity and connection is an illusion: "Looking close, you saw that under the thick ivy each house had something distinctively its own. Some touch that was Gothic, Romanesque, baroque or Greek triumphed amid the Victorian clutter" (1). This is not a simple celebration of diversity, however, as "they all shared the same brown monotony. All seemed doomed by the confusion of their design" (1). This is an uneasy confluence of sameness and difference, one that reads as confused.

Indeed, the brownstones in general and the one that the family inhabits in particular are representative of how things change but also how the past continues to haunt the present. The narrator identifies the "Dutch-English and

Scotch-Irish who had built the houses" as being mostly absent by the time the narrative begins in 1939, either "discreetly dying behind those shades or selling the houses and moving away" (2). Their place is taken by West Indians, who the narrator describes as "like a dark sea nudging its way onto a white beach and staining the sand" (2). This simile is fitting because of the island origins of the population it describes, but it has notably negative connotations through the use of the word "staining," which suggests contamination. While these homes were likely meaningful to their original inhabitants, the novel suggests that they are particularly precious to the West Indian and especially Barbadian immigrants, who "had never owned anything perhaps but a few poor acres in a poor land" (2); their position as the descendants of the enslaved in a British colony still dominated by a white landowning class makes them acutely aware of the power that landownership holds. As a result, they "loved the houses with the same fierce idolatry as they had the land on their obscure islands" (2). Despite this intense dedication, the narrator notes that "the old houses remained as indifferent to them as to the whites, as aloof" (2). In other words, the intense dedication directed toward the houses is not only unreturned; it cannot be.

Significantly, the novel introduces the titular brownstones before there is a description of the titular brown girl. By establishing Selina's complex relationship with the house, which is "alive" to her (2), the novel sets up the central role this structure will have in her life. When we meet Selina, she is "a ten-year-old-girl with scuffed legs and a body as straggly as the clothes she wore," with "wide full mouth, the small but strong nose, her eyes set deep in the darkness of her face" (2). The physical description of Selina as an awkward tomboy is coupled with the ideas that Selina seems older than her years and, most notably, that she seems to "know the world down there in the dark hall and beyond for what it was. Yet knowing, she still longed to the leave the safe, sunlit place at the top of the house for the challenge there" (2). The house may be indifferent to her, but Selina is not indifferent to it; she sees it both as a site of comfort and a place she wishes to escape.

Selina uses her imagination to insert herself into the house's history, creating for herself a fiction of belonging:

> She rose, her arms lifted in welcome, and quickly the white family who had lived here before, whom the old woman upstairs spoke of, glided with pale footfalls up the stairs. Their white hands trailed the bannister; their mild voices imploring her to give them a little life. And as they crowded around, fusing with her, she was no longer a dark girl alone and dreaming at the top of an old house, but one of them, invested with their beauty and gentility.

She threw her head back until it trembled proudly on the stalk of her neck and, holding up her imaginary gown, she swept downstairs to the parlor floor. (3)

This flight of fancy sets up the fact that, for all of her eventual disdain for her mother's dream of owning the house, the brownstone gives her something meaningful. The confidence with which she walks as a result of imagining herself as a part of its grandeur is powerful. This fantasy also makes it clear that the whiteness of the previous owners is part of the house's power; the paleness of their bodies is emphasized, and she is transformed into "one of them," taking on the characteristics that she believes them to have had based on the memories of Miss Mary, the Irish Catholic former servant who lies slowly dying in the house of her former employers, surrounded by a new wave of immigrants. Of course, the novel rejects Miss Mary's depiction of the past as beautiful and genteel.

Selina's imagination allows her to feel that she belongs, but the reality of seeing herself breaks the illusion. In being faced by her physicality in the mirror, she realizes "that was all she was. She did not belong here" (3). Despite their absence, she still feels that the house "belonged to the ghosts, shapes hovering in the shadows" (4). The presence of the home's white former owners is more powerful than her embodied, current presence. This sense of unbelonging is, perhaps, what her mother's drive for ownership is meant to overcome, but the novel suggests that Silla's approach will ultimately be fruitless. The idea that home ownership will create belonging is based on a belief in capitalist logics that are a deeply embedded aspect of respectability politics and model-minority discourse. The adult Bajan women in the community, "the mother and the others" (8), are able to suck their teeth at and dismiss the "white children on their way to school [who] laughed at their blackness and shouted 'nigger¹'" (8) because their focus on their economic mission is so relentless: "Their only thought was of the 'few raw-mout' pennies; at the end of the day which would eventually 'buy house'" (8). These women have fully accepted the idea that to succeed in the US, they must break through a "glass-ceiling" (Ninh 11). Yet the women are not untouched by the indignities that they suffer. The narrator describes them as "those watchful, wrathful women whose eyes seared and searched and laid bare, whose tongues lashed the world in unremitting distrust" (8). Their defense helps them get through their days

---

1. The text as written has been retained. The author's use of this term is purposeful and relevant to the topic of this book, as the mockery these women receive is explicitly racial and does not differentiate between them and the African American women from whom they understand themselves to be separate.

of scrubbing floors, but it also shapes them into terrifying figures devoid of softness for the people in their lives, especially their children. They pay what Christian calls "the spiritual prices" that they believe to be necessary for economic advancement (82). Selina's fear of becoming like these women fuels her distrust of her mother's house-buying mission. If this is what it takes to buy a house—to thanklessly serve, to take abuse without talking back, to be in a constant state of antagonism with the world in a way that crushes your dreams and your ability to trust anyone—then the price is too high.

The novel is explicit in its critique of respectability and its role in the life of the children of immigrants. Selina's lover, Clive, provides a detailed sketch of the picture of respectability:

> Such as you went to one of these factories called city colleges, desperately trying to be the dark counterpart of the American coed and studying to be a teacher or social worker—or if your parents were more ambitious, a doctor or lawyer. If you were the oldest you played the piano badly, the second-born, the violin worse. Worn those ugly silver bangles since you were born practically. Religiously went to the hairdresser every two weeks. Belonged to the Episcopal Church, a Negro sorority and of course the [Barbadian] Association. That you were already looking around for a nice, ambitious West Indian boy, lighter than you preferably, whose life you could order. Dreaming already of the wedding that would end all weddings and settling down to the house, the car, the two clean well-behaved children. And, of course, you were still a virgin. (201)

This long and detailed laying-out of what is expected of young Bajan American women contains all of the key markers of both respectability and model-minority discourses as imagined in a highly gendered context: striving for middle-class income and values through working toward a respected professional career approved by parents, the desire to demonstrate "accomplishment" through British-defined traditional means like playing an instrument, and maintaining individual respectability through sexual purity followed by endogamy with a man who increases your status in the context of colorism. Respectability is characterized by the right membership in the right organizations, the right physical appearance that demonstrates willingness to conform to societal pressures by way of regularly having one's hair straightened, and obedience as well as allegiance to the family unit through wearing the silver bangles; above all, it is clear that how one is perceived is what matters most. erin Khuê Ninh argues that the immigrant family is a particular "production unit" that aims to produce good capitalist subjects (2), and this passage demonstrates that well, as the adherence to the expected path leads to capitalist accumulation as represented by an ostentatious wedding, a house, and a car. The "two clean well-behaved children" represent the continued production of this model in the next generation, solidifying the community's ascension to the middle class.

Of course, many children of immigrants do not meet these exacting standards. What are the parents to do when such "failure" takes place? Clive is not only the recounter of expectations; he is also the example of how it looks not to meet them. When telling Selina about the time his mother burned all of his paintings, he strives to articulate why he and his mother stay locked in a perpetual state of mutual dependence and conflict. Selina asks, "Why didn't she just disown you and throw you out?" and Clive replies, "Mothers? Hell, they seldom say die! Fathers perhaps. Like my poor father. He just acts like I don't exist. But not mothers. They form you in that dark place inside them and you're theirs. For giving life they exact life" (226). Clive accuses his mother and all mothers of being the prime architects of the systems of expectation and filial obligation that Morris and Ninh identify.[2] While Clive clearly has some contempt for his mother, and himself for being unable to resist her influence in his life, he nevertheless sees why this dynamic is so seemingly inescapable. When Selina asks, "Why, then, don't they just leave you alone?" he responds with compassion toward his parents: "Because it's a long haul and they need all of us. Because there are so few of us and so many of the whites, and they are so strong and contemptuous . . ." (227; ellipsis in original). Here, Clive articulates the bind that the second generation inhabits between their demanding parents and an unfriendly society. Ninh makes the astute point that

> while there is no question that the losses of immigration matter, that institutional racism and media representation figure into the second-generation experience, so too does power in the most intimate, vulnerable, and formative social contexts—one which may demand that the subject compensate for familial losses by successfully navigating hostile social and political waters, and which may very well redouble the stakes of "racial" failure. (5)

---

2. It is worth noting that there is a certain degree of misogyny built into Clive's character that shapes his worldview and that the novel subtly critiques. His difficult relationship with women is clearly meant to be shaped by his dynamic with his mother. As such, his comments that relate to gender should often be taken with a grain of salt. Yet his description of how mothers function here is in keeping with the novel's depiction of Silla and Selina's relationship and the overall structure of filial obligation that the novel is concerned with, so I take Clive's observations here to be earnestly represented rather than ironically so.

It is true that "the pressure to conform can thus be understood as a wish to protect and shelter the younger generation against an essentially hostile white world" (Japtok 311), and the immigrant family's aim to defend itself from the world around it through consolidation and control is a response to the very real threat posed by a racist society. But this approach requires sacrificing children at the altar of an unappeasable god: respectability.

When the children push back against this sacrifice through a desire to pursue their own interests and to eschew the rigid path laid before them, parents are forced to question the necessity of their approach. Clive makes this argument in relation to his desire to be a painter: "When we snub their way they begin to ask themselves: 'Can we possibly be wrong and they are right?—those fools with brushes?' Oh it's never conscious, but they've still got to get rid of that hidden doubt" (227). In other words, the rigor with which they police the boundaries of respectable behavior is the result of their own self-doubt, their fear that they did not need to sacrifice quite as much as they have for the goals that may not make them as happy as they want. This moment and the trajectory of the relationship between Silla and Selina builds the novel's critique of respectability as an understandable but ultimately insupportable means of protection from the dangers of American society.

The idea that the daughter must be a virgin is an aspect of respectability that is taken for granted to the degree to which it goes unquestioned, but this novel draws attention to the constructed nature of this standard through the character of Miss Suggie as well as through the contrast between the expectations applied to girls and boys. Ninh argues that the "prohibition against sex for the second-generation daughter" produces a "particularly gendered subject" (128). She points out that it makes sense that "it is the appearance of virginity rather than its fact that matters, if its primary function is not as economic resource but as a symbolic product of willing accommodation to power" (Ninh 142). The picture that Clive paints of the respectable Bajan American girl is capped off by an insistence on virginity precisely because she must ultimately give the impression of submissiveness even as she is expected to be active in her pursuit of material success and in her ordering of her eventual husband's life.

By contrast, the sexual promiscuity of Miss Suggie is seen by the community as rebellion against them even if that is not her aim. Miss Suggie tells Selina, "Yuh mother! Them so! My people! I's hiding from them with tears in my eyes. . . . Y'know what they want me to do? . . . I must put on a piece of black hat pull down over my face and go out here working day in and day out and save every penny. That's what. I mustn't think 'bout spreeing or loving-up or anything so" (67). Miss Suggie's complaint is that she wants to prioritize pleasure in her life, which she does not perceive as hurting anyone else, but the wider Bajan community refuses to leave her to her own devices. As King points out, there is a double standard of morality at work in the community's approach to Suggie in comparison to its approach to Deighton or Clive (369). The men of the community are blamed for their economic rather than moral failures, reinforcing a highly gendered set of expectations. Still, Suggie's perceived rebellion, like Clive's, forces the community to question their approach to things and such questioning is terrifying and must be suppressed. Miss Suggie shows Selina that an oppositional relationship to the community's taboos around sex is possible but also that such opposition is dangerous. Selina thus keeps her sexual relationship with Clive secret, abiding by the rules of respectability by maintaining the appearance of virginity.

While the novel is focused on Selina, the narrative provides meaningful insights into the psyche of her parents, whose conflict, as I have mentioned, shapes Selina's internal struggles. Selina loves her father excessively, not only because he provides her sweetness that her mother withholds but because he represents a freedom that she wants for herself. He goes out at night, dances, has extramarital affairs, spends hours during the day napping in the sun like a cat, and generally gives the impression of living for pleasure. His freedom, however, is an illusion that he is only able to maintain by remaining inactive. He continuously claims to be preparing to make his way in the world through efforts like taking a correspondence course in accounting, but it is indicated almost immediately that his approach sets him up for failure, as he states that he "ain even gon bother [his] head with all this preliminary work they sending now" and will instead "wait till they send the real facts and study them" in order to make good money so that he and Selina can move back to Barbados, where he can set himself up as an important person (9). His unwillingness to do the work means that when he is rejected for accounting jobs, having only applied at "the three places offering the best salary" (69), he is able to give up immediately and frame it as an act of masculine integrity.

When Silla points out that his approach shows that he does not really want a job, he argues, "I ain lookin for nothing small. I ain been studying this course off and on for near two years to take no small job. Tha's the trouble with wunna colored people. Wunna is satisfy with next skin to nothing," and asserts, "It got to be something big for me 'cause I got big plans or nothing a-tall. That's the way a man does do things!" (69). For Deighton, masculinity provides an ideal excuse for avoiding challenges and the reality of what it means to be a Black man in a racist society. His sense of masculinity requires that he see himself as equal to white men, and while this impulse is admirable, it results in him choosing to ignore the reality of how society treats people like him. By placing the blame on what "wunna colored people" accept, he sets himself up as an exception whose individual characteristics should make him exempt from the struggles that his wife and the rest of the Bajan immigrant community have to face. He is not, after all, unaware of the power of racism either in the US or in Barbados, as is clear when he whispers to Selina that "here and in Bimshire they's the same. They does scorn yuh 'cause your skin black"[3] (69). Nevertheless, he suppresses this knowledge so that it only creeps out when he is particularly depressed. Christian points out that "Deighton's desire to have everything or nothing results so often in his having nothing that his insistence turns into self-deprecation" (90). Deighton frames himself as an idealist, but the novel undercuts his self-representation through the narrative's observations on his deeper psychology. Beneath his bluster and his bitterness, there lies "a frightening acceptance, it seemed to be, which sprang, perhaps, from a conviction hidden deep within him that it was only right that he should be rejected" (69). Because Deighton is unwilling to look racism in the face, he is unable to see his own internalized racism and its role in his choices. The novel introduces several key characters through biting descriptions attributed to Silla, and the one for Deighton is perhaps the most accurate and the most damning: "But look at he. Tha's one man don know his own mind. He's always looking for something big and praying hard not to find it" (17). Selina loves her father for resisting to be pushed into the box that society has built for him, but part of her coming-of-age is realizing that the means by which he did so were perhaps just as damaging as the road chosen by his wife, Silla, because they required him to withdraw from life.

While her father is important to Selina's sense of herself and the world, the mother is even more powerful, perhaps precisely because Selina wants to resist her influence. Silla is a dreamer trying incredibly hard to be a realist, and this tension at the center of her psyche shapes how she sees herself and her relationships with those around her. In the argument that ultimately sends Deighton into the arms of the cult leader Father Peace and the alluringly simple and unambitious life he represents, Silla explicitly articulates the motivation that has been driving all of her actions in the novel, while at the same time defending herself from how others might see her, how she might even see herself: "'It's not that I's avaricious, or money-mad,' she whispered to herself, . . . 'Or that I's a follow-pattern so that everything they do I must do. But c'dear, if you got a piece of man you want to see him make out like the rest. You want to see yourself improve. Isn't that why people does come to this place?'" (149). As a woman, Silla's place in the world is in some ways dependent on her "piece of

---

3. Bimshire is a nickname for Barbados.

man," whether she likes it or not. Her improvement is tied up with his success. She is also right to point out that the purpose of coming to America is, at least according to both mainstream American and immigrant discourse, to improve your lot in life and gain some form of material success. Because she has embraced that mission, she belongs in America; because Deighton has not, Silla asserts that he "don belong here, mahn" (149). His lack of belonging is not just that he does not have success: "It's that you was always looking for something big and praying hard not to find it" (149). This assessment, while harsh, is accurate, which is precisely why it strikes true and pierces the "veil" that has shielded Deighton since his religious conversion. He does not want success, because deep down he does not believe that he deserves it or that he can handle it. Yet his sense of masculinity dictates that he must seem as though he is pursuing it. His ultimate failing as an immigrant, then, is that he has not sufficiently transformed internally into the true capitalist actor he needs to be to succeed.

Silla must continue to believe that she did what she had to do in order to live with herself after her husband's deportation and death. While Japtok reads her as representative of the "Old World ethnic community" (313), I argue that she is much more representative of Ninh's intervention, "which sees the immigrant for the opportunistic, survivalist *first-generation American* [s]he is—one whose relentless adaptation process is driven by the pragmatism of household governance, and the demands of thriving in capitalist America" (22). Her behaviors are more rooted in the realities of immigrant life in the US than they are based on her upbringing in Barbados, where a related but distinct set of social norms and hierarchies shaped her youth. Silla embraces a kind of capitalist fatalism, arguing that "nearly always to make your way in this Christ world you got to be hard and sometimes misuse others, even your own" (192). This thesis is based on the not inaccurate claim that "we would like to do different. That's what does hurt and shame us so. But the way things arrange we can't, if not we lose out" (192). This capitalist society may be unpleasant, but to work outside of it is an impossibility.

Silla's understanding of how capitalism works is based on a theory of power that sees racism as just one of its many manifestations: "No, power is a thing that don really have nothing to do with color. Look how white people had little children their own color working in coal mines and sweatshops years back. Look how those whelps in Africa sold us for next skin to nothing" (192). Part of what makes Silla such a compelling and repellent character is her ability to clearly see the ugly truth of capitalism and to articulate that truth, then to nevertheless embrace it. Silla is in many ways a prime example of Nietzsche's claim that "he who fights with monsters might take care lest he thereby become a monster. And if you gaze for long into an abyss, the abyss gazes also into you" (§146). Having gazed into the abyss of capitalism, she has been penetrated by it in return. Rather than seeing the distortion of values produced by the system of power that she describes and rejecting it, she argues,

> No, nobody wun admit it, but people got a right to claw their way to the top and those on top got a right to scuffle to stay there. Take this world. It wun always be white. No, mahn. It gon be somebody else turn soon—maybe even people looking near like us. But plenty gon have to suffer to bring it about. And when they get up top they might not be so nice either, 'cause power is a thing that don make you nice. But it's the way of this Christ world best-proof! (193)

The phrase "Christ world" is represented in the novel as a regular figure of speech, but its presence here is of particular importance because it draws attention to the fact that Silla's vision of the world is based on the idea of it as an inherently wicked place where engaging in sinful behavior is an inevitability.[4] In other words, she is capable of recognizing the corruption that results from hierarchy and domination but can only imagine that the way to overcome being at the bottom of such a system is to continue to reproduce it.

Selina is not willing, and perhaps not able, to fully give in to her mother's worldview, even as she sees it born out in various ways around her. Hearing her mother's pronouncements about the state of the world produces an internal struggle for her: "It was her own small truth that dimly envisioned a different world and a different way; a small belief—illusory and undefined still—which was slowly forming out of all she had lived" (193). Like Silla, Selina's perspective is shaped by her life experience. As the daughter who has witnessed how her mother's striving to grasp whatever small amount of power she can has caused unhappiness and destruction for them all, she cannot bring herself to embrace her mother's capitalist fatalism, even as she does not quite have the tools to concretely imagine an alternative. She muses that "then, too, the mother might be right," but this thought produces in her a visceral rejection: "That thought made Selina suddenly bear down on her lip until the skin

---

4. Michael L. Cobb argues that "there is something, then, about religious language, when uttered by Afro-Caribbean women, that gives their voice a particular kind of irreverent authority and, conversely, gives the rhetoric another kind of colour, another kind of semantic meaning that infuses the deadness of the white, religious words with another life" (643). This authority contributes to Silla's power as a speaker as well as the ambivalence that results from it for both other characters within the novel and readers.

almost broke, it fanned her rage and dread into a fierce heat" (193). Selina's anger at her mother's self-absolving belief is strong, but she cannot express it to her mother's face: "She turned, some angry word springing to her lips, only to die there as she found the mother's eyes fixed on her with their mute plea for understanding and tolerance" (193). In this moment, Selina intuits that her mother must believe her words in order to continue living with herself in the aftermath of the choices she's made. Ultimately, Silla's theory of power removes her sense of agency in a way that also frees her from responsibility. This devil's bargain provides her comfort but also feeds her daughter's hatred of her.

While, at the beginning of the novel, it is suggested that Selina understands the world outside, actually experiencing it changes how she thinks about herself and her family. Her life at college offers her a freedom she has not previously enjoyed, but it also brings her into greater contact with the white world, a world rife with danger for her. Indeed, it is in the aftermath of her greatest triumph that she most fully comes to understand what her Blackness can mean to others and how they can impose that meaning onto her.

Selina signs up for a modern dance class at the suggestion of her program advisor, where she befriends Rachel Fine, a young Jewish woman. Rachel also comes from an insular community with gendered and classed expectations of behavior. She has also experienced life as an outsider, as evidenced by the story of her blond hair: "It used to be very blond and long, and everybody was always saying I was like a little *goye* with my blond hair and blue eyes. Except, of course, the little *goyim* brats in school" (240).[5] Her brief story paints a vivid picture of her community's peripheral place on the edge of whiteness; she is valued within her community for the possibility that she can pass, even as her non-Jewish peers make it clear to her that they still do not see her as one of them. As with Selina and Silla's relationship, Rachel's own relationship with her mother is shaped by her mother's dreams of mainstream respectability, in her case the restoration of her blond hair and her marriage to a suitable boy. The young women bond immediately, and Rachel asks Silla to join the Modern Dance Club, of which she is president.

As she strays further from the insulating and suffocating embrace of her community, Selina becomes ever more aware of how people react to her presence. When telling Clive about her introduction at the club, she notes that

---

5. *Goye* is the feminine form of *goy*, which is Yiddish for gentile or non-Jew. *Goyim* is the plural form.

there was a "funny silence" and stalls out from describing it, stating, "You know the kind I mean" (217). The narrator notes that Selina is

> unable to describe the abrupt drop in their animated talk when she entered, the subtle disturbance in their eyes before they said hello. Nor could she describe her own feelings standing there; the sudden awareness of danger that made her hastily scan the room, a momentary desire to leave and thus spare them her unsettling dark presence; then, just as strong, the determination to remain . . . (217; ellipsis in original)

While Selina is unable to articulate her feelings, the narrative captures the powerful and contradictory response that wells up in her as she becomes aware of how she is perceived. Her body knows instinctively that she is in danger, and she is caught between the desire to protect herself and to assert herself. This experience is disturbing for her, perhaps especially because it is beyond articulation. Nothing has happened yet and there is indeed no guarantee that something will, but her body is not wrong that danger is possible if not likely.

What marks Selina as a rebellious daughter of both her family and of the nation is precisely that she chooses to remain. After all, she tells Clive, "What am I supposed to do—curl up and die because I'm colored? Do nothing, try nothing because of it?" (217). Her refusal is at first strong, but it wavers, going from an angry "I'm not going to do that!" to "I don't want to do that, Clive" as she notices his "tired expression and the small muscle pulling at his mouth" (217). Selina is still in the early stages of her engagement with the white world, whereas Clive has already been burned by it. His world-weariness is part of what attracts her to him, but it also fills her with anger and fear at times.

Clive responds thoughtfully to her conflicted emotions, although his response is tellingly colored by his own experience and his gender:

> "No," he said gently, "you can't do that because then you admit what some white people would have you admit and what some Negroes do admit—that you are only a Negro, some flat, one-dimensional, bas-relief figure which is supposed to explain everything about you. You commit an injustice against yourself by admitting that because, first, you rule out your humanity, and second, your complexity as a human being. Oh hell, I'm not saying that being black in this goddamn white world isn't crucial. No one but us knows how corrosive it is, how it maims us all, how it rings our lives. But at some point you have to break through to the large ring which encompasses us all—our

humanity. To understand that much about us can be simply explained by the fact that we're men, caught with all men within the common ring." (217)

On the one hand, Clive acknowledges that Selina is right, that she must keep doing things despite how others perceive her or treat her. He acknowledges that to give in to the fear, to withdraw for the sake of others' discomfort at one's "unsettling dark presence" (217), is giving into the idea that one's race is all that one is and that one has an unchanging place in the world solely based on one's Blackness. On the other hand, he asserts a universalizing vision that is predicated on the understanding that "we're men, caught with all men within the common ring." The gendered nature of this statement is not incidental; he is only able to understand racism through the lens of his experience as a Black man specifically. He tells Selina, "Who knows what they see looking at us? . . . Some of them probably still see in each of us the black moor tupping their white ewe, or some legendary beast coming out of the night and the fens to maraud and rape. Caliban. Hester's Black Man in the woods. The Devil. Evil. Sin. The whole long list of their race's fears" (218). All of his specific examples are explicitly masculine. So, while Clive plays an important role in Selina coming to better understand how her race shapes her experience of the world, his insight is limited, and she must reach beyond it to set her own course through the choppy waters of America's racial hierarchy, which so deeply intersects with its systems of gender construction.

It is within this same conversation that Clive both articulates a version of respectability politics and asserts that he has opted out of it. After paraphrasing "Jimmy Baldwin" to say that white people fear Black people because they fear what they do not understand within themselves, he states, "But I'm afraid we have to disappoint them by confronting them always with the full and awesome weight of our humanity, until they begin to see us and not some unreal image they've super-imposed" (218). At first glance, this does not look wholly like respectability politics, as it is focused on the fullness of Black humanity as opposed to the construction of an idealized and acceptable version of it, but it is still based on the belief that white people can be convinced of Black people's humanity through the actions of Black people. The onus is still on Black people to display themselves in order to produce a desired result. Clive believes this is necessary, but he also refuses to do it: "'This is the unpleasant and perhaps impossible job and this is where I bow out, leaving the field to you, my dear sweet odd puritan Selina'—he prodded her playfully—'and to the more robust among us. Me, I can't be bothered. To hell with them. I'm assured of my humanity lying here alone in this goddamn room each day seeing things in my mind that I can't get down right on canvas'" (218). Clive refuses to engage in respectability politics, but this refusal has not freed him.

Clive may be assured of his humanity, but he is unable to express himself and to truly pursue his passion for painting. He believes that only someone like Selina, whose self-control and strength he both admires and is shamed by, are capable of continuing to break through the veil, to use the language of Du Bois. Clive claims that he "tried once" and tells the story of a well-meaning white friend, who "was always asking [him] how it felt to be colored" (219). Clive's realization that he had never succeeded in proving to this friend that he was "anything other than a Negro" led to both the end of their friendship and Clive's decision to no longer try, not just to protect himself but seemingly for the comfort of white people as well: "He was trying. And why hurt people when they're so damn fragile inside . . . ?" (219). This diagnosis of "white fragility" a half century before the term gained popular usage by way of the work of Robin DiAngelo is significant here because it identifies a core problem with respectability politics as a means of contravening liberal white racism. It is something internal to the white friend that makes it impossible for him to see Clive as more than his color, something that no amount of Clive's behavior can change. It is that same internal characteristic that produces in Selina the instinct to "spare them her unsettling dark presence" (217). In essence, white fragility both demands that Black people abide by respectability politics and cannot stand to actually see Black people succeed in abiding by it because of the psychological and ideological challenge such success poses.

In her relationship with Clive, Selina is unwillingly recreating her mother and father's relationship. Clive is in many ways like Selina's father, particularly in his instinct to disengage, which is part of what draws Selina to him as well as part of what forces them apart in the end. Selina seems incapable of choosing the resentful passivity that the men in her life embrace. Clive is aware of this, even if Selina resists this idea. He tells her often that she will leave him, stating that he knows this because "people like you who seize hold don't need my type, not for long" and telling her that when she seized him, it was not him that she was taking hold of but "life itself by the throat" (213). Selina is shocked and horrified by his characterization of her because it makes her think of her mother: "This was the mother's way!—which had seemed so opposed to her own small yet undefined truth, which had so infuriated her" (213). Here, Selina is forced to realize that "her oppositional course might have brought her full circle to the ruthless pursuit of goals that is her mother's mark, even though their goals may differ" (Japtok 310). Selina cannot disengage like Clive and her father, but neither is she willing to fully embrace her mother's ruthless approach to life. The novel demonstrates her stumbling path toward a different approach, one that is active, unlike her father, and asserts her own agency, unlike her mother.

The climax of the novel is also the interaction that most explicitly draws together the threads of respectability politics and model-minority discourse and that demands that Selina directly confront her own version of the realization that Clive had with his friend who could only see him as his Blackness. The night of the Modern Dance Club recital, Selina gives a powerful and excellent performance. The novel suggests that its power comes from her old soul: "The huge eyes in her dark face absorbed yet passionate, old as they had been old even when she was a child, suggesting always that she had lived before and had retained, deep within her, the memory and the scar of that life" (243). This could be read as an allusion to a kind of postmemory, as theorized by Marianne Hirsch, inherited from her enslaved and colonized ancestors and expressed through art. In Selina's dancing of the life cycle, she draws on both her own experiences as well as those of others around her, including the priest in her sister's church and Miss Mary dying in her bed (243). In essence, her dance is a full and undeniable demonstration of the richness of her humanity and her engagement with the rich humanity of others. If it were possible to convince others of one's humanity, this dance would have surely achieved that goal. The novel's detailed representation of this performance is crucial to the events that come afterward because of how clearly it demonstrates the paradox described above that makes the achievement of respectability so threatening to whiteness despite the demand for it.

The dancers congregate for an after-party at the home of Margaret, whose mother subjects Selina to a masterclass in liberal white supremacy. The woman—as she is referred to throughout the scene—summons Selina to come see her in the other room. The novel foreshadows the significance of this scene at the very beginning of their interaction, through Selina's rumination on the woman's carefully arranged "courteous, curious and appraising smile": "Months, years later, Selina was to remember it, since it became the one vivid memory of the evening, and to wonder why it had not unsettled her even then. Whenever she remembered it—all down the long years to her death—she was to start helplessly, and every white face would be suspect for that moment" (246). This interaction is a turning point for Selina that fundamentally shapes her relationship with white people for the rest of her life. The woman's physical paleness, embodied in her skin, hair, and eyes, reveals that "something fretful, disturbed, lay behind their surface and rove in a restless shadow over her face" (246). In this scene that is so defined by the woman's view of Selina's Blackness, it is the woman's whiteness that is most tangible: "Selina could *feel* her whiteness—it was in the very texture of her skin" (247).

Despite this, Selina does not at first understand that the woman is her adversary. When the woman asks Selina how it feels to be the star of the show, Selina answers genuinely and freely. The narrative, however, conveys the woman's various microexpressions, noting her smile stiffening when Selina refers to relying on her imagination (247). What, after all, is more utterly human than imagination?

The woman finally begins to show her hand in a way that Selina recognizes when she asks if Selina lives uptown (247). When Selina tells her no, she is from Brooklyn, this leads to one of the most ubiquitous and oft-explored aspects of immigrant and second-generation experience: the "where are you from" conversation. Writing about the experience of being asked these kinds of questions, Sara Ahmed points out that "these questions only appear to be questions; they often work as assertions," arguing that the one being asked where they are from is made questionable by the asking (Ahmed, "Being in Question"). This element of assertion comes through to Selina because of the question's delivery and its undercurrent: "It was not the question which offended her, but the woman's manner—pleasant, interested, yet charged with exasperation" (248). The woman's desire for mastery over Selina is the root of this exasperation; she is displeased that she does not already feel that she can fully categorize and file Selina away.

The woman is triumphant when she finds out that Selina's parents are from the West Indies, saying, "Ah, I thought so. We once had a girl who did our cleaning who was from there . . . Oh, she wasn't a girl, of course. We just call them that. It's a terrible habit . . . Anyway, I always told my husband there was something different about her—about Negroes from the West Indies in general . . . I don't know what, but I can always spot it" (248; ellipses in original). Here, she directly asserts the model-minority status of West Indians, as in contrast to African Americans. Her relief that she correctly assessed Selina to have a Caribbean background comes from the way in which she is able to maintain her view of African Americans and the limitations she believes them to have by policing the boundary between Black people from elsewhere and Black people from the United States. She goes on to tell Selina, "You don't even act colored. I mean, you speak so well and have such poise. And it's just wonderful how you've taken your race's natural talent for dancing and music and developed it. Your race needs more smart young people like you" (249). Here, she once again asserts Selina's difference while also reinforcing that this supposed difference does not remove her from being subject to a stereotyped and condescending view of her Blackness. She is both not like other Black people in her speech and carriage as well as just like other Black people in that she is the recipient of a natural facility that is the result of her Blackness. The woman can take comfort that Selina is a better dancer than her daughter because Selina has a natural and unfair advantage as a result of her African ancestry; she is simply developing something that she has, and therefore her hard work is less impressive. The woman, then, is articulating a belief in primitivism as a means of putting Selina in her place while seemingly praising her.

The term *primitivism* refers to the "adoption of motifs, subjects, and styles associated with primordial, elementary, fertile, or preindustrial qualities" in art by those who wish to rebel against the "'exhausted' values of mainstream Western civilization" (Heinrichs 992). It is not solely associated with African and African diasporic people and art, but in the early twentieth century this reading of the legacy of Africa within African Americans was a powerful force both amongst Black people and the white audiences who were attracted to their work. Because believers in primitivism thought that Black people had a primordial connection to Africa, a place that they understood largely through stereotype, colonial imagery, and myth, Black art could be read through the lens of this "natural" affinity to the things they associated with Africa, like rhythm, simplicity, connection to the natural world, and sensuality. This is how it was possible for extremely complex and modern forms like jazz to be thought of as primitive. For African American artists, the turn to primitivism could be a gateway to a greater connection to a previously denigrated ancestry; white audiences, however, could mobilize primitivism to continue to other and isolate Black art and Black people, as the woman does to Selina.[6]

The woman legitimizes her claim for the model-minority status of West Indians and the rightness of her thinking about Black people in general by invoking her West Indian former servant: "Ettie used to say the same thing. We used to have these long discussions on the race problem and she always agreed with me. It was so amusing to hear her say things in that delightful West Indian accent" (249). It is, of course, obvious why Ettie would always agree with her employer about the nature of the "race problem": her employment depended on it. Ettie is one of "the mother and the others" (8), keeping her head down and pleasing her employer to save the money she needs. Whether or not Ettie's real opinions were in alignment with the woman is unknowable. It serves the woman's best interest to see Ettie as a willing interlocutor even as she must know that her control in their relationship makes such a thing impossible. Through her politely delivered cavalcade of condescension, the woman seeks to assert herself over Selina just as she did over Ettie and just as she believes she has the right to do over all Black women,

---

6. Langston Hughes's short story collection *The Ways of White Folks* contains several stories that thoughtfully and hilariously critique primitivism, written at the time when the ideology was still very much in vogue.

West Indian and otherwise. Her differentiation between West Indian Black folks and American Black folks is not, therefore, born out of recognizing cultural and historical distinctions but rather a useful tool to wield against both groups. Japtok rightly points out that Selina's confrontation with the woman demonstrates that her color shapes how she is read more than her ethnicity, which "serves as a kind of 'Americanization' in that it blurs ethnic distinctions" (311). As such, this confrontation contributes significantly to the novel's critique of model-minority discourse by revealing the lie behind the Bajan community's belief that distancing themselves culturally from African Americans can protect them.[7] The woman's differentiation between West Indian Black folks and American Black folks does not make her racism any less pernicious or powerful.

This interaction is the catalyst for Selina's realization of "the full meaning of her black skin" (250). Rosamond King brilliantly identifies this interaction as "one of those racist interactions that is insignificant because of the smallness of the person, slightly veiled because of its politeness, and yet devastating because of its ontological violence" (374). Until this point, Selina's struggles had been most overtly with her family and her community; it is not that she was unaware of the dangers of the larger world so much as she had yet to truly face it for herself. Ironically, she has been shielded from these dangers most of all by the mother (Troester 13), even as that relationship has also been a source of pain. Selina experiences this realization as a kind of death: "And knowing was like dying—like being poised on the rim of time when the heart's simple rhythm is syncopated and then silenced and the blood chills and congeals, when a pall passes in a dark wind over the eyes" (250). It is fitting that the description is so focused on the body. This moment could be read as the death of her innocence, but more accurately it is the death and rebirth of her relationship to her body because it reveals to her the irreconcilability of her self-image with how she is perceived in the world. She wonders why the woman cannot see "that she was simply a girl of twenty with a slender body and slight breasts and no power with words, who loved spring and then the sere leaves falling and dim, old houses, who had tried, foolishly perhaps, to reach beyond herself?" (249–50). This passage emphasizes that Selina is a young woman coming of age through its description of her body. The narrative is insistent of her embodiment, her sensuality, and her subjectivity, even as it reveals these things to be not enough to defend her against the power of the white gaze.

---

7. Long before this section, the novel has established the affective value of greater connection with African Americans through the figure of Miss Thompson, a migrant to New York from the South, who serves as a loving and wise mentor for Selina, what Troester calls an "othermother" (13).

The recognition that her self-perception cannot penetrate racism fills her with terror. It also reveals to her that she had already internalized the racism that she is confronted with long before she was able to articulate it to herself: "And obscurely she knew: the part of her which had long hated her for her blackness and thus begrudged her each small success like the one tonight . . ." (250; ellipsis in original). In this moment, Selina is forced to acknowledge that she has inherited some of her father's character after all. She has not escaped the self-hatred that the American racial hierarchy actively works to instill in Black people, even though she has managed to suppress it enough to live her life. This is why it is significant that the woman's eyes are described as "a well-lighted mirror" (250); in seeing this hatred directed at her from the outside, Selina is forced to uncover it within herself, which is an even greater experience of suffering than to feel it from another.

The novel concludes this scene of devastation with one of the most powerful articulations in literature of the stakes of white supremacy for the individual Black person. Selina, having fled the apartment, confronts herself against a glass wall:

> It was no use. Exhausted, she fell against the glass, her feverish face striking the cold one there, crying suddenly because their idea of her was only an illusion, yet so powerful that it would stalk her down the years, confront her in each mirror and from the safe circle of their eyes, surprise her even in the gleaming surface of a table. It would intrude in every corner of her life, tainting her small triumphs—as it had tonight—and exulting at her defeats. She cried because, like all her kinsmen, she must somehow prevent it from destroying her inside and find a way for her real face to emerge. Rubbing her face against the ravaged image in the glass, she cried in outrage: that along with the fierce struggle of her humanity she must also battle illusions! (252)

This passage powerfully expresses the inescapability of racism and white supremacy. Here, she fully confronts what her father spent his life trying to suppress his own knowledge of and what her mother has let herself be consumed by. In so doing, the novel suggests that the only way out is through; there was no way for her to move forward without this confrontation and without this breakdown. Despite the gut-wrenching nature of this scene, where she publicly succumbs to the sorrow and anger that are the result of truly internalizing an unwanted reality, by going through it, the rebellious daughter does what neither of her parents were ever able to achieve: a full and conscious recognition of her condition combined with the fire to resist it actively.

Nevertheless, the above realization is what makes it possible for her to finally empathize with the mother. Her own despair gives her a new kinship with the women she previously scorned: "And she was one with them: the mother and the Bajan women, who had lived each day what she had come to know. How had the mother endured, she who had not chosen death by water?" (253). She acknowledges here that the mother's decision to stay took courage that her father did not have. The novel is explicit in its valuing of the sacrifice that the mother made but also the ways in which that sacrifice scarred her. Selina asks herself how her mother had contained her "swift rages," only to remember that her mother had not in fact contained them: "And then she remembered those sudden, uncalled-for outbursts that would so stun them and split the serenity of the house" (253). The image of the immigrant mother suffering in silence for her children is so common as to be unquestioned, but Marshall refuses to look away from the reality of immigrant mothers as real human beings who experience real consequences as a result of their sacrifices. Selina reflects that "the mother might have killed them. For they were the ones who drove her to that abuse each day, whose small faces reflected her own despised color" (253); the parent-child dynamic depicted here is one where the child is the reflection of the parent and, however inadvertently, the source of the parent's pain. If the mother did not have her daughters to care for, would she have endured all that she had? Would she have needed to harden herself so much against the world if she had not had more than herself to protect? Nevertheless, the novel makes it clear that the suffering of the mother does not mean that the daughter must submit to the mother's will.

Selina plans one rebellion: winning the scholarship by "pretending" to be a respectable young woman (an act that is, basically, actually being a respectable young woman, with the exception of engaging in discreet sexual activity) and then using the funds to run away with Clive and reject her community's ways. But the rebellion she actually enacts—publicly confessing her plan and refusing to take the money—is far more devastating to the community because it is honest and forces community members to confront the artificiality of their own standards and the integrity required to reject them. Selina tells the Association that she cannot accept the scholarship, "not only because [she doesn't] deserve it, but because it also means something [she doesn't] want for [her] self" (262). By refusing the scholarship, Selina escapes being indebted to the community for her freedom.

This is the first of several dual rebellions, or, more accurately, combinations of failed and successful rebellions explored in this book. Frequently, protagonists discover that rebellion looks different as they come of age, that true rebellion demands an honest reckoning with the reality of what is being rejected, not just its most obvious form. Onstage, Selina tells the crowd, "My trouble was maybe that I wanted everything to be simple—the good clearly separated from the bad—the way a child sees things" (262); her maturation has forced her to recognize that while her conflict with the Barbadian Homeowners Association is legitimate, it is not because they are bad and she is good or even vice versa. Instead, she must face the complexity of both herself and her community, must know that by choosing to alienate herself from the "familiar faces," she must also become "aware of the loneliness coiled fast around her freedom" (262). In representing Selina's rebellion, Marshall asserts that the sacrifices necessary to achieve her freedom are worth it, but she refuses to downplay how significant those sacrifices are.

In Selina and Silla's closing confrontation, Silla explicitly mobilizes the idea of filial obligation to try to convince Selina not to leave. Silla says, "Going 'way. One call sheself getting married and the other going 'way. Gone so! They ain got no more uses for me and they gone. Oh God, is this what you does get for the nine months and the pain and the long years putting bread in their mouth . . . ?" (264–65). erin Khuê Ninh argues that "the construct of 'filial obligation' defines the parent-child relation as a debtor-creditor relation, but within the system without contract or consent, the parent-creditor brings into being a child-debtor who can never repay the debt of her own inception and rearing" (16). Here, Silla is staking that claim on her daughters, arguing that by giving birth to them and feeding them, they owe her their continued presence and fealty. Silla's lamentation affects Selina, but not enough to sway her: "And although Selina listened and felt all the mother's anguish she remained sure" (265). In this moment, she tries to show her mother empathy without capitulation.

This choice to stand steadfast against her mother's evocation of debt sets her apart from Clive, who she leaves precisely because he is unable to overcome his guilty feelings enough to choose his lover over his mother (256). As Barbara Christian points out, Clive is able to articulate what has him stuck, in a way that Deighton could not, but he is still incapable of unsticking himself (101). Silla states that Selina scorns her for her desire to buy a house, and Selina replies honestly: "I don't scorn you. Oh, I used to. But not any more. That's what I tried to say tonight. It's just not what I want" (265). This exchange is powerful because it demonstrates a transformative againstness that has brought Selina closer to her mother while freeing her to go her own way. She has finally come to terms with the fact that she is very much like her mother: "Everybody used to call me Deighton's Selina but they were wrong. Because you see I'm truly your child. Remember how you used to talk about how you left home and came here alone as a girl of eighteen and was your own woman? I used to love hearing that and that's what I want. I want it!" (265). Selina has finally been able to make the crucial distinction between what she loves and what she is. She recognizes that like her mother, she is ambitious and independent, and that her desire for Clive, like her love for her father, is based on being attracted to difference rather than similarity. Silla is a prime example of Susana Morris's contention that "novels frequently portray female characters who question or struggle with adherence to the ideals of respectability politics, yet persist in policing others' behavior under the same rubric" (9). Silla has spent Selina's life applying standards to her that she herself has never succeeded in meeting. In finally coming to terms with how similar she is to her mother, Selina frees herself to choose a path that can embrace those aspects of herself, without feeling condemned to repeat her mother's mistakes. She is not doomed to be her mother if she continues to acknowledge her own agency and breaks the pattern of holding others to a standard she cannot meet herself.

This moment of mutual recognition between mother and daughter is not a moment of full reconciliation in the sense that the two women realize how they can get along. Instead, by seeing herself in her daughter, Silla is able to let Selina go: "'G'long,' she said finally with a brusque motion. 'G'long! You was always too much woman for me anyway, soul. And my own mother did say two head-bulls can't reign in a flock. G'long!' her hand sketched a sign that was both dismissal and a benediction. 'If I din dead yet, you and your foolishness can't kill muh now!'" (266). As I will argue throughout this book, sometimes it is both necessary to work to understand one's immigrant parents and to simultaneously distance oneself from them. As I have written elsewhere, "the act of recuperating complex and painful familial dynamics does not always take the form of family reunion" (Jeffers 1). Silla's claim that "two head-bulls can't reign in a flock" demonstrates that she has also had to confront the similarities between herself and her daughter, even the ones she was hoping to avoid, and though her goodbye is ambivalent—as both "dismissal and benediction," it too reflects the push and pull of *against* at the heart of this book—it is a gift to her daughter insofar as it releases Selina to disappoint her.

Selina closes the novel in turmoil but determined to forge a new path for herself, however unclear that path may be. She has rejected the respectability that her mother dreamed of for her, and she has seen firsthand that to be a model minority is a poisoned chalice that keeps one forever subordinate to white people even if it raises one over others. She is cognizant that she is about to face a hostile world. The final image of the novel is Selina throwing one of her two bangles—bracelets strongly tied to her Bajan identity as well as her femininity—into a construction site, "a vast waste—an area where blocks of brownstones had been blasted to make way for a city project" (268). If the brownstones can be read as the hopes of the West Indian immigrants who believed that owning them would solidify their place in the nation, this construction site is the demolition of those dreams. Throwing the bangle is, therefore, another deeply *against* act; she does it to "leave something with" all of the people that she's ever known (268), making it a gesture about both leaving and staying connected. She is giving up some of her heritage, though not all of it since she keeps the second bangle, in a way that symbolically makes it a physical part of the city, to be buried beneath the new city project, an artefact for future generations. Selina has rejected a house and, in some ways, the idea of a home, leaving her perpetually living against her family and her place of birth.

Paule Marshall's *Brown Girl, Brownstones* serves as an indictment of both the respectability politics and model-minority tactics within the immigrant community it represents and the racism of the society around that community. The novel does not shy away from how these twin pressures, one from within and one from without, limit the sense of agency girls and women feel themselves to have. It also asks readers to seriously consider the sacrifices that come with choosing rebellion against both of these systems, especially because rebelling against the suffocation of the self-protecting immigrant community can also mean placing oneself at the mercy of a fundamentally unwelcoming society. Through the character of Selina, Marshall makes clear how the daughter of Black immigrants is not shielded from racism by her outward adherence to the expectations placed upon her. As the earliest rebellious daughter explored in this volume, Selina sets the stage for decades of daughters who must navigate the double bind that Marshall so powerfully lays out in this novel.

CHAPTER 2

Rebelling against Repetition

In Edwidge Danticat's powerful debut novel, *Breath, Eyes, Memory*, the protagonist Sophie's therapist pushes her to answer whether she has ever hated her mother for the incredible pain she caused her. Sophie tells her therapist, "I can't say I hated her" (207). The therapist counters that she does not want to say it, and Sophie replies that she will not say it, because "it wouldn't be right, and maybe because it wouldn't be true" (207). Sophie Caco, the daughter of a Haitian immigrant to the United States, whose mother took her away from the loving home she grew up in with her aunt in Haiti, finds herself unwilling and maybe unable to maintain the estrangement between herself and her mother that was established by her first overt act of rebellion: breaking her hymen with a pestle. Her rebellion is a terrible act of self-harm that she sees as the only way out of an untenable situation with her mother. Her journey throughout the rest of the novel is one of reconciling with both herself and her mother in order to try to free herself from the trauma that shaped their lives and offer a better future for her own daughter. As I trace the nature and role of rebellion throughout this book, I see Danticat's novel as adding important complexity to an understanding of rebellious Black immigrant daughters, as they reject respectability and model-minority practices in ways that can benefit or harm them. This novel reveals the importance of enacting a nuanced reading of rebellion, as Sophie's most overt rebellion serves to reproduce the traumas of the past, while her more subtle form of rebellion—speaking what is usually kept silent—is what creates the possibility of a better future. At the same time, this novel demands that readers sit with the necessity of Sophie's rebellions and asserts that the suffering of the daughter at the hands of a mother who has herself suffered be taken seriously in its own right.

In the introduction, I noted that the debtor-creditor relationship between immigrant parents and their children that erin Khuê Ninh describes makes it difficult for the daughter, at least the dutiful daughter, to see her life as her own. As Ninh writes, "the construct of 'filial obligation' defines the parent-child relation as a debtor-creditor relation, but within the system without contract or consent, the parent-creditor brings into being a child-debtor who can never repay the debt of her own inception and rearing" (16). This dynamic in immigrant families produces the conditions for daughters who feel both obligated toward and resentful of their parents in a way that may be more intense than in nonmigrant families. A few years after being expelled from her mother's home for presumed sexual misbehavior and, therefore, having failed in her obligation, Sophie returns to Haiti, as does her mother, where they reconcile, only to have their tentatively renewed relationship cut short by the mother's unplanned-pregnancy-induced suicide.

Sophie's rebellion is a direct result of her migration and her reunion with her mother. She is a very well-behaved girl when she is living with her aunt in Haiti. As Sophie is departing to join her mother, Tante Atie tells Sophie, "I would like to know that by word or by example I have taught you love. I must tell you that I do love your mother. Everything I love about you, I loved in her first. That is why I could never fight with her about keeping you here. I do not want you to fight with her either" (20). Tante Atie frames Sophie's obligations as based in love, and because Sophie does love her, she agrees, promising that she will not fight with her mother. But while her relationship with her aunt is based on love and a history of direct care and intimacy, the source of her responsibility toward her mother is less clear. Tante Atie rightly points out that "in this country, there are many good reasons for mothers to abandon their children" (20); the capitalist structures that produce the need for migrant labor produce affective effects such as the estrangement of mother and daughter that is present in this text among many others. In the novel, the effects of this estrangement are heightened by the fact that Sophie is the result of her mother's rape.

The power of the mother over the direction of the daughter is a given even under these circumstances. Despite their emotional distance, Sophie's mother, Martine Caco, states her expectations of her daughter in the cab on the way from the airport: "You are going to work hard here . . . and no one is going to break your heart because you cannot read or write. You have a chance to become the kind of woman Atie and I have always wanted to be. If you make something of yourself in life, we will all succeed. You can *raise our heads"* (44). Sophie is expected to lift her whole family through being a hardworking good girl as defined by her mother. While this expectation is so common in immigrant contexts as to be unremarkable, it is nevertheless an example of her mother's power over her life and her direction. Martine's expectations are an example of Ninh's argument that within the immigrant family, "power [features] in the most intimate, vulnerable, and formative social contexts—one which may demand that the subject compensate for familial losses by successfully navigating hostile social and political waters, and which may very well redouble the stakes of 'racial' failure" (5). Sophie is expected to justify and compensate for all her mother's decisions and suffering by fulfilling her mother's dreams for herself.

Martine's own life does not adhere to the image of respectability toward which she pushes her daughter. The dissonance between the reality of Martine and Sophie's lives and Martine's desired, imaginary version of those lives creates the damaging behaviors that Martine visits upon her daughter. Martine is a prime example of Susana Morris's argument that "Black women's writing also depicts the strains of family relationships beneath the façade of stability and respectability. Novels frequently portray female characters who question or struggle with adherence to the ideals of respectability politics, yet persist in policing others' behavior under the same rubric" (9). While Martine's rape is by no means her fault, her position as a single mother, one who did not raise her daughter for the first several years of her life, puts her outside of the bounds of respectability. Yet she maintains an investment in it by forcing it upon her daughter, who she sees as an extension of herself and therefore a means by which she can rewrite herself into respectability.

Martine has a specific and often intractable sense of what is "proper" despite how distant this propriety is from her own life experiences. When Sophie lies to her mother about being interested in a Haitian boy, her mother states that "it's always proper for the parents to talk first. That way if there's been any indiscretion, we can have a family meeting and arrange things together. It's always good to know the parents" (79). This normative perspective bears no resemblance to her own life as a single mother, as an immigrant, as a woman in a relationship in a country in which neither her parents nor her boyfriend's parents live. Martine's later actions, including the sex with her boyfriend that leads to her tragic second pregnancy, are overt examples of how she is unable to live up to the standards that she tried to enforce upon her daughter. Crucially, the novel does not condemn Martine for not living up to the standard she enforces; as Morris points out, the novel instead "compels a critique of the paradox of respectability, for the Cacos hold a stern allegiance to the ideals of respectability politics while finding it impossible to actually conform to these ideals" (75). Her flaw is not her failure of respectability; her flaw is that she imposes this damaging standard on her daughter.

The strangest indication of Martine's expectation of control is through the presence of the life-size doll in her apartment. The doll is everything she wants her daughter to be, even those things that she cannot be: she is tall, well-dressed, "caramel-colored with a fine pointy nose" (44), and, crucially, silent and pliable. It is clear that Martine treated the doll as her daughter before she brought her daughter to live with her. She anthropomorphizes the doll, telling Sophie, "We will show you to your room," with the "we" referring to herself and the doll (44). Martine says that the doll is like a friend and kept her company while they were apart (45), a claim that foreshadows Martine's neediness and her inability to accept that Sophie will not be as passive a "friend" as the doll has been. The doll is also representative of Martine's own arrested development into an adult as a result of her trauma, a lack of maturity that is not opposed to but rather deeply responsible for her dominance over her daughter. Martine gives Sophie the doll in this scene, without asking her if she wants it. Sophie initially attempts to share her bed with the doll, however uncomfortably, but there is not enough room for both of them in the bed (46). Her mother removes it from the bed, giving her more space, but then places the doll carefully in the corner. In now taking the doll's place in the bed but not expelling the doll completely, Sophie takes on its former role with the added pressure of the doll's presence as a reminder of the idealized version of her that her mother constructed for herself.

At this stage in the novel, Sophie chooses not to rebel against her mother's expectations, despite her discomfort. She chooses to accept her new situation, looking in the mirror her first day in New York: "I greeted the challenge, like one greets a new day. As my mother's daughter and Tante Atie's child" (49). This distinction is significant; her connection to her mother is one of explicitly gendered expectations and a traditional familial relationship, while her connection to Tante Atie is based on love and trust. In her role as daughter, she feels unable to tell her mother when she is afraid and uncomfortable. At the same time as she is getting to know her mother, she is thrown into an unwelcoming American school system that her mother gives her dire warnings about: "My mother said it was important that I learn English quickly. Otherwise, the American students would make fun of me or, even worse, beat me. A lot of other mothers from the nursing home where she worked had told her that their children were getting into fights in school because they were accused of having HBO—Haitian Body Odor" (51). Sophie is subject to the xenophobia of her peers, and it is her responsibility to overcome it through quickly learning English. These circumstances are a revealing example of the confluence of respectability politics and the politics of migration. In the same way that Martine enforces the virginity cult as the arbiter of a girl's worth, she also submits to the idea that immigrants must conform quickly in order to be treated fairly by their peers. As in the case of respectability politics when it is tied to sexuality, she is not incorrect that other children may treat immigrant children poorly if they are unable to speak English well, but her warnings reveal both a propensity to blame the victim and an uncritical conflating of unrelated reasons as to what, precisely, will incur the negative treatment that she wants to avoid; speaking English fluently will not protect Sophie from being perceived as having "HBO."

The novel also highlights how media representation of the AIDS epidemic contributes to anti-Haitian sentiments (51); despite their significant differences from each other, both the idea of HBO and the mainstream association of Haitians with AIDS can only be escaped through a thorough form of assimilation, not just through linguistic proficiency. After all, Sophie and her peers are subject to mockery for attending Maranatha Bilingual Institute by the kids at the public school across the street, but this is just as much tied to their being "the Frenchies" as it is to their being perceived as "boat people" and "stinking Haitians" (66). Linguistic difference is just a tool in the arsenal of discrimination, not the source of it. The role of smell in how immigrants are identified and ostracized is present in much immigrant fiction across racial lines and is a prime example of how difference or the perception of it is rooted in the body not just in terms of how it looks but its other sensual characteristics. Accusations of smelling badly are powerful because they represent a layer of scrutiny that destabilizes self-perception in a complex way; if you smell how you have always smelled and how the people you are most commonly around smell, you are generally unaware of these scents, so to have this aspect of yourself called out is jarring both because it asserts a different reality than the one you previously experienced and it marks as contemptible something you are not certain you are able to identify. Although it is possible, changing how you smell is much more difficult than changing how you dress or do your hair. This often leads to hypervigilance about smell among immigrants. Moreover, the "reality" of how one smells is not really the issue when it is associated with an ethnic signifier in the way that "Haitian Body Odor" is—smelling thus becomes as an intrinsic characteristic rather than something changeable and circumstantial. Once again, the means by which one could be protected from this perception is through no longer being read as Haitian.

Yet such assimilation is rife with danger because becoming unmarked as immigrants for these Black Haitians is to become indistinguishable from Black Americans, an association that Martine is not keen on. Martine sends Sophie to a Haitian Adventist school (65) and tells her not to trust "those American boys" (67), which is implied to be specifically in reference to African American boys. Martine is also still deeply entrenched in a Haitian understanding of social hierarchy, as can be seen by her perception of her own relationship, which she values because of Marc's higher-class status in Haitian terms (59). Sophie also knows instinctively to tell her mother that the boy she is interested in is Haitian when she is trying to hide her relationship with her future husband, Joseph (79), perhaps because Martine just assumes that Sophie's only options are and should be choosing between "old-fashioned Haitians and the new-generation Haitians" (80). It is clear that integration with the African American community is not Martine's aim.[1] Indeed, Martine's understanding of status is classically immigrant in the sense that it combines social precepts from her home country with the American dream narrative. She tells Sophie that "in Haiti if your mother was a coal seller and you became a doctor, people would still look down on you knowing where you came from. But in America, they like success stories. The worse off you were, the higher your praise. Henry's mother had sold coal in Haiti, but now her son was going to be a doctor. Henry's was a success story" (80). Martine is attracted to the idea of social mobility in the US, and this social mobility requires careful adherence to practices associated with respectability and model-minority identity that limit her daughter's self-determination.

Sophie's mother has complete control over what she should be—a good girl—and how she should be it: by dressing a certain way, becoming a doctor, and not having a boyfriend until she is eighteen (56). When her mother's boyfriend asks what she wants to be when she grows up, Sophie responds, "I want to do *dactylo* . . . be a secretary" (56). Martine rejects this, asserting, "She is too young now to know" and dictating to her that she will be a doctor. Unlike immigrants from parts of the anglophone Caribbean and West Africa, Haitian immigrants are rarely if ever considered to be "model minorities"; indeed, at the time the novel was written, they were often characterized as particularly undesirable migrants in media and popular discourse because of the aforementioned association with AIDS as well as the broader framing of the Haitian body as "a site of state conflict and (continued) violence"

---

1. As Tara T. Green points out, the novel itself works against this separatist perspective and instead "challenges readers to expand their idea of African American or black to be inclusive of the multiplicity of the experiences and histories of all people of African descent rather than to restrict it to a U.S.-centered one" (82).

(Alexander 96). Yet Martine's pronouncement demonstrates that she is working within the same "success frame" that Jennifer Lee and Min Zhou describe in relation to Chinese and Vietnamese working-class communities (39); the internalization of model-minority practices does not require being generally perceived to be a model minority. Part of what classifies this form of ambition as a model-minority behavior as opposed to a respectability behavior is that it functions outside of usual American class expectations. That is, immigrants striving for the professions are perceived differently from working-class African Americans striving, in so far as immigrant striving is perceived as a natural by-product of their positionality, as opposed to being in defiance of it. Sophie's mother's insistence that she should become a doctor is a classic immigrant parent trope, but this conflict between their two dreams for her life also serves a meaningful metaphorical purpose. Doctors heal and *dactylos* transcribe; Sophie does both through her story. As she documents the trauma and the resilience of her mother line,[2] she works toward healing herself through speaking and confronting that which has been kept silent and hidden. Sophie therefore fulfills her mother's wish for her life in spirit but not in letter; she does not what her mother wants but what both she and her mother need.

Sexuality is a central area of conflict in narratives of rebellious immigrant daughters. Familial control over a daughter's sexuality is a hallmark of patriarchal power everywhere, even as it is wielded by women. In *Breath, Eyes, Memory*, this form of control is enacted through the practice of "testing," when a mother uses her fingers to check that her daughter's hymen remains unbroken. This act of violation is represented as being common in Haiti and exemplifies a cult of virginity that values women solely based on their supposed purity. Morris rightly points out that this virginity cult is "not simply an exaltation of chastity but a cultural fixation on women's bodies and sexualities parading as a glorification of purity" (76). Sophie's grandmother and her mother see it as both their right and responsibility as mothers to keep their daughters "pure" for their future husbands. Under this worldview, consensual sex is a violation while nonconsensual intimate touching by family is a justifiable cultural practice. Many scholars have pointed out the way that testing is deeply tied to rape (see Counihan; Gerber; Francis); the practice both mimics and claims to prevent it. The novel makes a direct connection between this way of approaching girls' bodies and the naturalization of sexual violence and denaturalization of sexual pleasure.

---

2. Danticat uses the term *mother line* to refer to her familial heritage in matrilineal terms. Because the family she depicts is made up entirely of women, the representation of lineage is focused on mother-daughter relationships through the generations.

Sophie embarks on her first romantic entanglement in the context of her mother's control over her sexuality. When Sophie meets Joseph, she is attracted to the fact that he "looked like the kind of man who could buy a girl a meal without asking for her bra in return" (68). In other words, his nonpredatory nature is what draws her. Nevertheless, she also recognizes that her mother would never approve; that "a good girl would never be alone with a man, an older one at that" (72). Their gentle and chaste courtship—they don't even kiss until after he has said he wants to marry her—is deemed sordid by her mother, who begins to test her after she comes home late one night.[3] Her mother justifies her actions by recasting Sophie's budding romantic relationship as a betrayal of their familial relationship: "The love between a mother and daughter is deeper than the ocean. You would leave me for an old man who you didn't know a year before. . . . You are giving up a lifetime with me. Do you understand?" (85). Her mother has unilaterally set the terms of their relationship, and, as Ninh asserts, "the meaning of a daughter's sexual conduct is determined not by the features of the act, but by the whim of the sovereign" (150). When Sophie is young, Martine claims that Sophie can have a boyfriend when she is eighteen (56), but Martine's behavior when Sophie actually reaches that age demonstrates that she is not willing to relinquish control over her daughter just because she has reached the age of majority.

The arbitrary nature of Martine's power is what makes it possible for her to move the goalposts in this way. Ninh draws on Giorgio Agamben's theorization of sovereign power to demonstrate that filial guilt is structural and that the immigrant parent, as the sovereign in the familial structure, "traces a threshold between that which is inside and that which is outside of the law . . . 'producing' his subject as such [the child], as well as deciding from among the activities of living what may fall under governance" (43). As the above scene suggests, this power is menacing because it is wielded by someone who is otherwise deeply powerless; Sophie is the only area in Martine's life where she holds significant power, which seems to make her wielding of it more erratic and more desperate. At this point, Sophie has only kissed, but this act is translated into abandonment by her mother. While discussions of daughterly chastity are often framed around a relationship to men, particularly the need to save the daughter's virginity for a future husband, Martine here reveals that this is not truly her concern. She sees Sophie's relationship, sexual or not, as an abandonment and feels it is her right as mother to punish Sophie's attempt

---

3. Gerber characterizes Martine's decision to test Sophie as a "post-traumatic stress response" (190). That reading is obviously quite sympathetic toward Martine but is not incompatible with the point being made here: that her behavior, whether an active decision or a post-traumatic stress response, is rooted in patriarchal ideologies and the desire for control.

to separate herself from her mother's power. This is not to say that Martine does not truly believe that a woman's value is tied to her sexual purity; this is made clear when she becomes pregnant and hears her unborn child call her "a filthy whore" (217). Nevertheless, this belief works in tandem with her desire to maintain control over her daughter.

While some might assume that an all-female family might be a safer space for a young woman's sexual agency, this novel makes clear that this assumption would be incorrect. Ninh's argument that "if authority figures both male and female take such an active investment in perpetuating this system, then authority figures both male and female must stand to gain from the successful production of specifically gendered daughterly subjects" (129) is supported by Sophie's confrontation with her grandmother. Sophie asks why mothers test their daughters, and her grandmother replies, "If a child dies, you do not die. But if your child is disgraced, you are disgraced. And people, they think daughters will be raised trash with no man in the house" (156). Here, Grandmè Ifé appeals to the absence of male authority as her reason for testing her daughters. She goes on to point out the social consequences of "failing" to maintain her daughters' purity: "If I give a soiled daughter to her husband, he can shame my family, speak evil of me, even bring her back to me" (156). Sophie keeps pushing, and her grandmother states explicitly, "I had to keep them clean until they had husbands," but, as Sophie points out, "they don't have husbands" (156). The supposed future beneficiaries of Grandmè Ifé's policing of her daughters' virginity never materialized. Through this explanation, Grandmè Ifé shows herself to be "entrenched in an especially egregious manifestation of respectability politics" through focusing on what she perceives to be men's desires and through "using folklore and mother wit to suppress dissent among women" (Morris 75). At the same time, these justifications demonstrate that the underlying concern that she is expressing is the decrease of her own social power, reputation, and freedom. Patriarchal power is the structure that facilitates her actions, but her own investments are what instigate her actions. Morris characterizes this as kyriarchy, "a system of power and domination that consists of multiple intersecting structures of oppression" in order to "emphasize how even those who are marginalized and have little social power or individual agency can broker power in ways that ultimately reify the larger constructs of domination in society" (81). Grandmè Ifé's kyriarchal behavior further contextualizes Martine's actions throughout the novel, as she re-enacts not only the physical activity of testing but the structure of power between mother and daughter that testing is the most egregious manifestation of. Sophie insists that her grandmother know that her actions continue to have consequences.

Sophie's choice of how to escape her mother's control is an extreme example of contradictions at the heart of being against. Ninh points out that "it is common to assume that a daughter has sex in defiance of her parents because the rewards of sexual relations or activity are such as to outweigh for her the cost of her family's grief" (152) and then shows how the texts she discusses reject this presumption. I argue here that Danticat's novel does as well. Sophie enacts her sexual rebellion not through actually having sex but by breaking her hymen with a kitchen implement, a pestle, from which she gains no pleasure and in fact injures herself badly enough to need stitches. Sophie sees this act as the only thing that will free her from her mother's power; she chooses to "fail" the test and be exiled rather than choosing to leave herself. She is caught in the system of designated failure described by Ninh. In this way, her rebellion is both terrible and strangely partial in that she is willing to defy her mother through inflicting upon herself an echo of the violation that stopped her mother from having to receive the "tests" from her own mother, which gives her mother the responsibility of casting her out rather than running away herself.

This choice to harm herself and break her mother's heart aligns with Ninh's argument that with "preservation of the family's well-being having been core to the doctrine of social obedience, the infliction of grief is less unfortunate by-product than naïve logical inversion: one must protect the family to be filial; one must harm the family to be free" (152). Harming the family here must also include harming the self; Sophie's freedom must come at a price to herself because she is functioning under the logic that "an 'unfilial' child should suffer, that surely the world will not countenance a daughter to flout parental will and meet no misery" (Ninh 153). The pestle is a phallic object, but it is also associated with domestic labor; just as she rebels against her mother by echoing her trauma, she rebels against a specific domestic vision of her life with an instrument of that domestic world. Sophie's rebellion is one of ironic inversions. By working within this system, Sophie frees herself from direct parental control but not from the trauma that shapes her mother's life. While she is engaging in what seems to be an overt act of rebellion, she is actually increasing her kinship with her mother even as she becomes estranged from her. As Gerber notes, this is expressed metaphorically through the story of the woman who will not stop bleeding, a story that represents both mother and daughter and "reveals the extent to which Sophie is enmeshed with Martine" (190). In this way, she is in a state of intense againstness; she is rebelling against her mother by becoming more like her, by holding her even closer through recreating her trauma.

Rebellion via self-harm also demonstrates how thoroughly she has *internalized* her identification with her mother. She is unable to lash outward, no matter how much her mother hurts her. At the same time, she understands instinctually that hurting herself will also cause her mother pain. This hurt is not the result of her mother's empathy—she is not suffering because her daughter is suffering—it is rather a result of the bind that she has made for herself as a result of her own traumas. The loss of Sophie's hymen is the loss of her respectability as well as her controllability, and Martine cannot fathom how to move forward without these two characteristics present in her daughter. Once Sophie has failed the test, Martine sees her leaving as inevitable: "She was calm now, resigned to her anger. 'Go,' she said with tears running down her face. She seized my books and clothes and threw them at me. 'You just go to him and see what he can do for you'" (88). In her mind, there is no way for Sophie to remain with her now that she has lost her respectability. Of course, Martine herself has been through an even more traumatic version of this same transition, but because she has never directly dealt with her own experience, she is unable to imagine a different outcome, perhaps one where control and love are not so completely intertwined. So, while Sophie's rebellion is partial, Martine reads it as complete.

Understanding that rebellion can take the form of self-harm is important because it highlights that a solely positive reading of rebellion does not reflect the complexity of it as a practice, especially in an intersectional context, where competing and combining forms of oppression create conditions that require an unimaginable deftness to navigate successfully. Knowing what one wants to reject is, regrettably, a great deal easier than knowing what one wants to embrace and, crucially, how to embrace it. Sophie does not want to be tested by her mother, does not want to live a fearful life disconnected from her own body, but what the alternative looks like is difficult to discern because of pressures and conditions in her life that are just as powerful as, or more powerful than, the behavior of her mother, pressures her mother is also subject to. Her upbringing has not prepared her for independence, so leaving her mother on her own does not seem to even enter her mind. Indeed, it is clear that simply going away to college would not be enough to remove her from her mother's power. Yet the rebellion she chooses does not seem to assert her agency: she forces her mother to cast her off, and she aligns herself with her soon-to-be husband's desires. Only when she has her daughter and returns to Haiti does she truly make a choice that she must drive herself.

Sophie inherits her mother's sexual phobia and, despite her attraction to her husband, she cannot bring herself to enjoy their sexual relations and instead disassociates during sex in the same way that she disassociated while being tested by her mother: "I had learned to double while being tested. I could close my eyes and imagine all the pleasant things that I had known.... After my marriage, whenever Joseph and I were together, I doubled" (155–56). Sex remains for her a necessary evil rather than a source of enjoyment. The unfulfilling nature of Sophie's sex life is revealed in her conversation with her grandmother. Early in the conversation, Ifé says, "crabs don't make papayas" (122), meaning that mothers produce children who are like themselves. The specific items she uses to express this sentiment are not without significance: the skittish, pincer-armed crab does not produce sweet and still offspring. When Ifé asks her if her husband is a good man, Sophie says, "He is a very good man, but I have no desire. I feel like it is an evil thing to do" (123). In this way, Sophie suffers from a problem that is ubiquitous in most if not all cultural contexts that overemphasize sexual "purity": she is not able to flip the switch from seeing sex as evil and dirty to seeing it as acceptable and even pleasurable just because she is married.

Even without the added complication of personal and familial histories of sexual violence, embracing sexual pleasure that was previously religiously condemned is rarely an easy or natural transition, as many women's personal testimonies and much research has revealed (see Fahs; Valenti; Klein). Sophie's sexual phobia is not, therefore, unique to her Haitian American context; as the previously cited authors suggest, white American evangelical Christianity regularly produces the same result. However, Sophie must confront the particular conditions that produced her sexual trauma in order to overcome it for herself and, in her mind most importantly, to protect her daughter from the cycle of sexual violence. Sophie loves her baby, but their relationship is not free from resonances of her past, which is symbolized through her appearance, as Brigitte looks like her grandmother Martine (101). Indeed, when Tante Atie says, "I cannot see this child coming out of you," Sophie agrees that sometimes she cannot see it herself (102). This feeling of distance is reflective of the strange, in-between space that Sophie inhabits with her body. At the same time, Brigitte's resemblance to Martine affords Sophie the strange opportunity to mother her mother, who failed to mother her.

Despite the suffering inflicted upon her by her mother and the ongoing effects of the sexual violation she experienced at her hand, Sophie cannot hate her mother, because she still feels a sense of filial obligation and because she has come to understand how her mother feels about her, through having her own daughter. She tells her therapist, "I feel like my daughter is the only person in the world who won't leave me" (210). I read this statement as an ambiguous moment; while Sophie does not want to have her named burned in a fire the way she has burned her mother's name as a cleansing ritual, will she be able to escape reproducing the same debtor-creditor relationship that led her mother to the acts that necessitated that burning in the first place? Since her rebellion against her mother simultaneously brought her closer to her mother through the echoing of their experiences of violation, her understanding of the mother-daughter relationship is shaped by her relationship with her own mother. How does Sophie's desire to keep her daughter close square with the novel's greater emphasis on letting go, as is clear from the final scene, in which Sophie finally faces her mother's trauma as a way of coming to terms with her death?

To approach these questions, I will now turn to Sophie's second rebellion: her refusal of silence. It is not without irony that Ifé is the one to tell Sophie, "Secrets remain secret only if we keep our silence" (123). While Ifé is the source of some of Martine's and, therefore, Sophie's sexual trauma through testing, she is depicted as having wisdom and love for her granddaughter that helps her. The coexistence of wisdom and damaging ideology, of love and harm, is a central theme of the novel and, indeed, of this monograph. The deep ambivalence that Sophie feels toward her grandmother and her mother is an aspect of the novel that needs to be sat with in a way that it rarely is. The desire to focus on her mother-as-victim or her mother-as-villain misses the opportunity to interrogate why we as readers might be so quick to recuperate or reject her mother when Sophie arguably does neither of these things. She mourns her mother, certainly, she seeks a kind of symbolic revenge on her behalf, but the novel does not end with her being "okay" with her mother or her mother's legacy. Seeing that there are some relationships that can only be healed spiritually within one party is necessary in order to avoid betraying the daughter of immigrants character in our rush to forgive and recuperate the immigrant parent. Just as Sophie does not let her grandmother off the hook for practicing testing, we as readers owe it to Sophie to take her suffering seriously and to recognize her mother's agency in producing that suffering. Sophie, after all, must do this if she is going to avoid reproducing the same pattern she suffered from. This is why her self-inflicted rebellion is partial and why the novel ends with the potential for transformation rather than the fact of it; the test is how she raises her own daughter. To succeed in raising a daughter who will not burn her name in the fire, she must complete her true rebellion: telling her story.

This second and more successful rebellion, however still in process it is by the novel's end, occurs through Sophie making choices that reject silence, embrace interethnic solidarity, and accept the ambivalent relationship she has with her mother rather than run from it or pretend that everything is fine between them. These choices are active and represent a refusal to accept key aspects of respectability and model-minority discourses, particularly the requirement to be quiet, accommodating, and, crucially, only forward-looking. While the future is important, the injunction to only look toward the future inherent in these twin discourses is based on the erroneous idea that simply ignoring the past will result in a better future. After all, history and experience make it clear that keeping one's head down, adhering to strict and often ill-defined standards of purity, and refusing help from others have rarely prevented discrimination or violence, produced wealth, or ensured happiness, yet respectability politics and model-minority discourse demand that one acts as though these results are a likely outcome. Martine attempted to live up to and apply these systems but failed and was unable to live with this failure. Through her choices, Sophie attempts to set these standards aside.

The most obvious way that Sophie rejects silence is through going to therapy and taking part in a sexual phobia support group. Her therapist, Rena, is a Black American woman who is clearly invested in her African diasporic identity, as signaled by her initiation as a Santeria priestess and the "Brazilian paintings and ceremonial African masks" that decorate her office (206). The novel presents Sophie's experience of therapy as somewhat ambivalent in that she and her therapist seem to have a tense relationship at times. Rena is represented as offering insight into her life and helping her to think differently about her mother than is her instinct, but she also takes on a scolding tone with Sophie and does not seem to always understand where Sophie is coming from, as when she asks the question "Did you have a chance to reclaim your mother line?" (207). Sophie replies that her mother line was always with her, revealing a cleavage between how Sophie and her therapist conceptualize connection. For Rena, the mother line has unequivocally positive associations that can be separated from the experience of mother-daughter conflict. For Sophie, the mother line is present and a more ambivalent force; it is not separation from the mother line that is her problem but rather her relationship to it.

Nevertheless, the narrative strongly supports the therapist's view that Sophie must confront the site of her conception. During their session, Sophie tells Rena that she ran past the cane field where her mother was raped, and the therapist replies, "You and your mother should both go there again and see that you can walk away from it. Even if you can never face the man who is your father, there are things that you can say to the spot where it happened. I think you'll be free once you have your confrontation. There will be no more ghosts" (211). Her claim prefigures the final events of the novel, although as I will explore more later on, the degree of her freedom at the end of the novel is a topic of much critical debate.

Perhaps the value of therapy in the novel, more than the answers and analysis provided by Rena herself, is the opportunity for Sophie to speak about her experiences in a way that she cannot do otherwise. Their discussions are in a context where Sophie is capable of talking back—a practice she was not raised to engage in. Sometimes this talking back comes in the form of defending those who wronged her, as when she states that it is hard to be angry at her grandmother because "after all she was only doing something that made her feel like a good mother" (208). But because readers, unlike the therapist, have witnessed the confrontation between Sophie and her grandmother firsthand, the way that Sophie is downplaying the interaction is clear. As such, therapy has obviously helped her express herself better, even if she does not always acknowledge it.

Narratively, these therapy sessions allow the novel to explicitly address the novel's themes, especially the ways in which Sophie struggles with extricating herself from the shared identity and trauma inherited from her mother. When Rena asks her to imagine her mother in the sexual act, she imagines her mother suffering through it, trying to "be brave." Rena astutely notes, "Like you" (210), pointing out the way that Sophie is projecting her own inability to enjoy sex and simultaneous simulation of enjoying it onto her mother. This creates a looping effect, as Sophie has come to experience sex this way because of her mother, and so by projecting this experience of sex on to her mother, she completes the terrible circuit. Therapy helps to identify the circuit as the novel goes on to explore how it might be broken.

It is important that Sophie's therapist is a Black woman and that her sexual phobia group is made up of women of color. The other two group members are Buki, "an Ethiopian college student" who is the victim of female genital mutilation (FGM), and Davina, "a middle-aged Chicana" who "had been raped by her grandfather for ten years" (201). All of these women share a history of migration, a form of sexual abuse by family, and the desire to take control of their own lives in the face of these struggles. The solidarity among them plays an important role in Sophie's journey precisely because all three of them are speaking the unspeakable. Like testing, FGM and incest are maintained by injunctions against girls and women speaking up for themselves and the belief that a girl's body is not her own. Their sexual trauma is particularly powerful because it comes from being betrayed by their most intimate relations. By working through this trauma in a group setting, they are combatting the loss of intimacy through the decision to actively choose intimacy with others who have experienced the same loss. They are not just choosing to speak, they are choosing to listen to each other, to form bonds that thoroughly reject the grounds on which they were victimized in the first place.

They attempt to process these betrayals through a mix of therapeutic means including burning the names of their abusers with a candle's flame, releasing a green balloon, and speaking prayers and mantras. Their mantras are about reclaiming their ability to control the narrative of their own bodies—"We are beautiful women with strong bodies"—but, crucially, they also emphasize the value of empathy: "Because of our distress, we are able to understand when others are in deep pain" (202). The decision to recognize not only your own pain but the pain of others is diametrically opposed to the harsh judgment of the self and others enacted by Martine. Rather than take up this same attitude, Sophie chooses to see her mother's pain: "I knew my hurt and hers were links in a long chain and if she hurt me, it was because she was hurt, too" (203). Sophie's decision to extend empathy to her mother is a rebellion because it transforms her mother from sovereign to human being; it is through this empathy that she is able to stop feeling guilty about burning her mother's name in the fire. Acknowledging her mother's hurt allows her to acknowledge her own and let go of the image of how a woman "should" be that plagues her mother until her death. Sophie knows that her mother's abuse was the result of the abuse she herself had experienced and recognizes that she too is capable of repeating the cycle, of being one whose name will be burned in fire, if she does not address her trauma directly.

The novel does not, however, suggest that this breaking of the cycle is either easy or guaranteed. While Sophie does feel "a little closer to being free" (203) after sexual phobia group meeting, she later sees the green balloon they released caught in a tree near Davina's house. While they had "thought it had floated into the clouds, even hoped that it had traveled to Africa," it was actually "slowly dying in a tree above [her] head" (221). This discovery suggests that the symbolic gestures of release the women engage in have their limits. This moment comes after a session with Rena, who tells her, "I think you have a Madonna image of your mother. Part of you feels that this child is a testimonial to her true sexuality. It's a child she conceived willingly. Maybe even she is not able to face that" (220). Sophie comes by her inability to accept her mother as a sexual being honestly, since her mother refuses to accept herself as one. Sophie has not yet been able to fully extricate herself from the damaging sexual ethic that she was raised with, despite her efforts. Just like the balloon, she has not gone as far as she hoped. But, unlike the balloon, she has the ability to keep trying.

The novel's exploration of interethnic solidarity is not solely situated in the relationships between women. The novel questions the idea of a firm border between Haitian and African American identities while at the same time refusing to ignore cultural differences between the two. Sophie's relationship with Joseph represents both of these elements of the novel. When they are first getting to know each other, Joseph tries to bond over speaking a form of Creole and telling her about his Louisiana heritage (70). This moment speaks to the diversity of African American identities and the ways that different strands of the African diaspora share significant connections across geography. Significantly, he objects to her calling him American, saying, "I am not American. . . . I am African American." When she asks about the difference, he responds by saying, "The African. It means that you and I, we are already part of each other" (72). Apart from being a very smooth line by a man courting a woman, this is also a decisively pan-African statement that is a part of his appeal to Sophie.

Nevertheless, the novel does not shy away from considering the particularities of Haitian experience that are in contrast to mainstream American, even African American, life. After all, the exchange that sparks Joseph's objection to being called American was Sophie's pointing out that his statement that "It is okay not to have your future on a map. . . . That way you can flow wherever life takes you" is "not Haitian" (72). Here, Sophie is accurately pointing out that this idea that being a wanderer is not only possible but even good is a foreign idea to her community and, indeed, most immigrant communities, as it is based on a different relationship to place than is accessible to them. To Sophie, Joseph is representative of a kind of freedom that she did not have any real idea of prior to their meeting, but the novel makes clear that he cannot give her freedom; she must find it for herself. Nevertheless, her decision to be with an African American man is one of the earliest ways that Sophie resists the vision of her life put forward by her mother. Despite living in the United States, Martine lives in a primarily Haitian world, mostly leaving its bounds only to work, and even there, most of her coworkers are Haitian as well. Sophie, by contrast, seeks to maintain her connection to Haiti while embracing her position as a Black woman in America.

The novel's spiritual elements serve as an important showcase for the ways in which Sophie is tasked with reimagining her cultural and familial inheritance so that she can find a way to move forward for herself and her daughter. One figure whose complexity offers the possibility of a nuanced relationship with this inheritance is Erzulie, who is the most prominent spiritual figure within the novel. Erzulie is the Vodun goddess of love, who is often conflated with the Virgin Mary. She has different incarnations, each of which are very different from one another: historian Joan Dayan describes them as "Erzulie-Freda, the lady of luxury and love; as Erzulie-Dantor, the black woman of passion identified in Catholic chromolithographs with the Mater Salvatoris, her heart pierced with a dagger; and as Erzulie-ge-rouge, the red-eyed militant of fury and vengeance" (6). "Mater Salvatoris" means mother of the savior; that is the incarnation of Erzulie associated with the Virgin Mary. Erzulie is therefore a complicated figure who does not fit into any binary opposition. She is both a virgin and a goddess of love, she is prayed to by gay men and sex workers, she is not androgynous but distinctly feminine even as she marries both men and women, and she is associated with a variety of colors in a context of a strict color hierarchy. As in most religions that do not have a written core text, there is no canonical version of Erzulie so much as common associations with and ideas about her, and as in most polytheistic religions, Erzulie is not "good" or "evil" in a Judeo-Christian sense. She is above human understanding so her actions cannot be judged by human standards. Her flexibility of meaning allows her to be mobilized in different ways, and the novel suggests that she can be embraced as a figure of female power and connection, but to do so is an active choice, not an inevitability based on the bare fact of a female deity of this kind. When Grandmè Ifé expresses real regret for the pain she has passed down to her granddaughter, after having at first resisted acknowledging the gravity of her actions, she hands her a statue of Erzulie (157). She is offering the statue as comfort, and Sophie takes it that way, clutching it to her chest as she cries all night; this moment also serves as a symbolic passing-down of the right to claim and even define the meaning of Erzulie. The cultural and spiritual order that Grandmè Ifé came from believed that Erzulie could exist alongside practices like testing and the idea that women exist to serve the needs of men, but in the hands of Sophie, perhaps a different understanding of the same spiritual figure can emerge. The possibility of this reformation of meaning is demonstrated by Sophie showing the statue of Erzulie to the members of her sexual phobia group (202). At this point she has not decided what meaning the statue will have for her family, but she sees it as having a place in her journey forward.

The last time Erzulie is invoked in the novel, it is in the context of Martine's burial. Sophie decides to dress her in a bright red suit, saying, "It was too loud a color for a burial. I knew it. She would look like a Jezebel, hot-blooded Erzulie who feared no men, but rather made them her slaves, raped *them*, and killed *them*. She was the only woman with that power" (227). Here, she imagines an Erzulie who is a straightforward inversion of the tyrannical power men have had over women, who is identified with the Biblical queen who is set up as the polar opposite of the Madonna figure that Rena accused Sophie of identifying with her mother. I do not believe that this passage, rooted as it is in Sophie's extreme grief at the sudden loss of her mother, with whom she was slowly becoming more reconciled, is meant to suggest that this inversion is a preferable final form of Erzulie. Indeed, this vision is still rooted in a Madonna/whore binary that flattens out the nuance of female sexuality and associates sexuality with domination. Moreover, Erzulie is still "the only woman with that power"—her singularity places her in the position to be the exception that proves the rule. Instead, I read this passage as Sophie trying to imagine her mother as having a kind of power in death she never had in life.

Sophie ends the novel in open defiance of the respectability and model-minority expectations imposed on her by her mother as she mourns for her mother. At her mother's funeral in Haiti, she makes a spectacle of herself; she externalizes her pain; she confronts the physical site of her mother's trauma head-on. By doing so, she engages in a final act of rebellion that is neither the self-defeating, intimate rebellion of the pestle nor the slow, intimate rebellion of speaking where there was silence; by running from the funeral to confront the cane field, Sophie takes her rebellion fully public, finally directing her physical rebellion outward. Significantly, as she fights the cane, the cane fights back. The cane field is not a neutral space. The cane field is the site of the death of her grandfather, her mother and aunt's childhood labor, and her mother's rape; in essence, her family's experience of the cane field shares the same characteristics as slavery: the loss of family, physical and economic exploitation, and sexual violence. This legacy of slavery shapes the family's present and cannot be truly confronted when abiding by the rules of respectability, which require a sweeping under the rug of past wrongs. By having the cane resist her assault, the novel suggests that this battle against the ancestral and recent trauma that has shaped her life cannot be easily won.

There is much scholarly debate about just how free Sophie is at the end of the novel. Her grandmother tells her that she will know the answer to the question "Ou libéré?," which translates to "Are you free?," but Sophie does not actually provide an answer in the moment (234). Some scholars, such as Nancy F. Gerber and Donnette Francis, argue that her confrontation with the cane finally fully frees her. Francis asserts that Sophie "frees herself from the debilitating subjection implicit in the previous scenes. Sophie's actions here must be understood as her will-ful re-membering of devastations enacted upon the bodies of her family members" and that the final scene constitutes "an act of healing" (87–88). Others, such as Semia Harbawi and Clare Counihan, see her freedom as only partial or suggested but not explicitly achieved. Counihan argues that "Sophie does not in fact succeed in speaking for herself: her 'Ou libéré!' remains unspoken, reflecting the text's ambivalent desire to formulate a Haitian identity that will both testify to Haitian history and function untraumatized in new diasporic spaces" (37). I argue that this novel speaks to the idea that freedom is a continuous practice, not a destination or a state. After all, the phrase "Ou libéré?" is framed as a regular part of speech for market women. It is not a question you only ask once. The novel therefore does not represent a Sophie who is finally and forever free; it demonstrates a Sophie who had begun the process of choosing to make herself free and has taken another significant step in that process through this moment of physical confrontation and spiritual engagement.

A powerful aspect of this final moment, however, is the way in which her grandmother publicly supports her rebellion. While her grandmother is still unable to confront fully the loss of her daughter—"her eyes avoiding the coffin" (232)—when Sophie attacks the cane, Grandmè Ifé not only does not try to stop her, she prevents the priest from doing so (233). The narrative turns to the communal and the intergenerational in the end. The Cacos come from a place where "nightmares are passed on through generations like heirlooms" (234); the novel seems to suggest that publicly facing the sources of these nightmares, recognizing their truth, is an important aspect of bringing about their end. Grandmè Ifé, like her mother line in general, is a source of both comfort and pain. As she joins Sophie in the cane field, placing a hand on her shoulder, she asserts a continued spiritual connection between Sophie and her mother even as she states that "there is a place . . . where the daughter is never fully a woman until her mother has passed on before her" (234). This suggests a cosmology whereby Martine is not only freed from pain by her death; her transition to ancestor will allow Sophie to become a full adult in a way that Martine herself never did. As such, Sophie's relationship with her mother does not end with her mother's death so much as it transforms, and this transformation will help rather than hinder her process of claiming freedom. Her grandmother's support in this moment suggests that death is not the only way that this transformation is possible, but the novel does not shy away from the idea that in Martine's case, her inability to direct her anger and recrimination outward made it impossible for her to continue to live.

Grandmè Ifé narrates a future conversation between the passed-on Martine and Sophie in which Martine tells a story and then asks, "Ou libéré? Are you free, my daughter?" and Ifé prevents Sophie from answering, placing her fingers over her lips and saying, "Now . . . you will know how to answer" (234). I read this moment not as Grandmè Ifé preventing Sophie from speaking, as Counihan has posited (46), but rather as Grandmè Ifé acknowledging that this is an exchange that must take place between Sophie and her mother, not between Sophie and herself. Grandmè Ifé is narrating a future event, one for which Sophie is still in the process of preparing. This proposed supernatural conversation with her dead mother indicates that while she is not, in this moment, free, because she is still in the cane, she has finally made it possible for herself to truly leave it. Answering "Ou libéré?" in this moment to this person is not the point. Sophie must turn to the future, a future of which her mother is still a part, but in a different form.

The paragraph that gives the novel its name expresses the kinship between mother and daughter in a way that reframes their relationship through a clear-eyed recognition of her mother's pain rather than a self-directed reproduction of it. Sophie narrates, "My mother was as brave as stars at dawn. She too was from this place. My mother was like that woman who could never bleed and then could never stop bleeding, the one who gave in to her pain, to live as a butterfly. Yes, my mother was like me" (234). To be brave as a star at dawn is to be resolute in one's place as one disappears from sight; here, Sophie embraces the reality of her mother's complexity. She also reorients how she thinks of her mother: "Yes, my mother was like me" (234). This is, of course, a strange turn of phrase. Her mother, after all, came first. But I read this statement as Sophie's choosing to see their likeness rather than taking it for granted and leaving it unspoken. In this unflinching look at their likeness, she can choose how to engage with it in a way that orients her toward the process of freedom.

Breath, Eyes, Memory depicts the multifaceted nature of rebellion. Ultimately, the novel offers a path forward for Sophie that requires that she remain in a state of againstness: to continue the process of choosing to be free, she must both embrace her mother and reject her mother's approach to life. Her first rebellion was partial because it naively recreated her mother's experience in a way that brought them closer together in pain but further apart in understanding. Her second, more productive rebellion, choosing to speak that pain to herself, her family, her therapist, and those who shared similar experiences, began the process of healing her relationship with her mother and herself. Her final rebellion, to eschew respectability, to publicly and freely confront the past physically as well as spiritually, is the culmination of her previous efforts but it is also not the end of that process. The novel's future-oriented ending makes it clear that the process of choosing freedom is not and will never be over. Jessica Marie Johnson refers to women of African descent "practicing freedom when they could not call themselves free" (12); although Johnson is writing about the eighteenth century, this formulation is precisely what Sophie does. In this way, she is carrying on a legacy of her Haitian ancestors even as she tries to bring an end to another, damaging legacy. Though Sophie's daughter is absent in this last scene, her significance cannot be overstated: the stakes of Sophie's rebellion do not just concern herself. If she is going to stop passing on nightmares like heirlooms, if she is going to avoid having her name burned in the fire, she must be a different kind of mother than the ones she has seen. This rebellious daughter must become a mother who does not compel the same kinds of rebellion. Sophie is a rebellious daughter because she will not accept the inevitability that her position as a woman, as a Black person, as coming from a proletarian background, as an immigrant, condemns her to a future of recreating the past. In the context of this project, Danticat's novel serves as a stunning example of how texts concerned with the daughters of immigrants can navigate in nuanced ways what it means to be a part of a family that is the source of both comfort and suffering, belonging and alienation. This novel's portrayal of a Black immigrant family beset by intergenerational trauma does not valorize the US as a site of freedom, but it does suggest the value of the interethnic—including pan-African—solidarity that is possible there.

CHAPTER 3

Self-Destructive Rebellion

In Taiye Selasi's 2013 debut novel, *Ghana Must Go*, one of the rebellious daughters of the Sai family reflects on the performative nature of her rebellious image: "An overachiever only playing at temptress, an ex-goody-two-shoes in bad girl footwear. It was a show, the vintage dresses and American Spirits, the rapid-fire wit and implied sex appeal, with learned lines and sharp costumes and dull supporting actors; she was playing at sex but knew nothing of love" (136). Here, Taiwo sees her transition from dedicated performer of "African Filial Piety" (233) to femme fatale who sleeps with the married dean of her law school as the move from one performance to another; neither represents some sort of intrinsic truth about her. Meanwhile, her younger sister, Sadie, sees herself in contrast with Taiwo, conceiving them as "mismatched siblings, the one dutiful, fair-to-middling if affable. The wind beneath. The other the bird" (150), all while meticulously maintaining and attempting to hide her bulimia. Yet, despite Sadie's view of herself as unrebellious in contrast with Taiwo, both daughters engage in the againstness this volume explores. Both daughters are rebellious, and both direct their rebellion inward, but one enacts a form of self-sabotage that is semi-hidden—an eating disorder—which saves her from the public downfall experienced by her sister as a result of her more overt acts of impropriety.

Ghana Must Go explores the reconnection of the Ghanaian and Nigerian American Sai family following the death of their estranged patriarch. Unlike the first two novels addressed in this book, *Ghana Must Go* offers not just one coming-of-age narrative but several through the depiction of the four Sai children, two girls and two boys. Focusing on the Sai daughters, I argue that this novel carries out a nuanced exploration of the tension between the model-minority characterization of African immigrants and the experience of American racialization for the second generation. The novel's depiction of how the immigrant desire to silence the colonial and difficult past, as a way of protecting and freeing their children, is potentially well-meaning but ultimately disastrous and even, in the end, cowardly, because it does not give them the tools to see how their parents' experiences and their own are a part of a continuum rooted in global white supremacy. In analyzing the different and at times self-destructive nature of the daughters' rebellions, I also argue that the silencing of the past leads to the misdirection of rebellious instincts against the self rather than in a more empowering direction.

The idea that rebellion is always practiced for the good of the rebel is fundamentally inaccurate, especially in cases where what is being rebelled against has multiple and fraught meanings for the rebel. Some rebellions are targeted inward so that they become masochistic in nature; erin Khuê Ninh describes how some rebellious daughters engage in "self-destruction as a means of self-preservation" (Ninh 116). She draws on Michelle Masse's argument that masochism is an "adaptive behavior" (Masse 51) through which "the masochist offers her own fantasy to ward off a worse dream or reality" (Masse 47). I argued in the last chapter that Sophie engaged in two forms of rebellion in *Breath, Eyes, Memory*, one of which was an act of self-harm. In this chapter, I explore two more cases of self-harming rebellion, but whereas Sophie's growth came through a second, externally directed rebellion, Taiwo's and Sadie's growth comes from a return to familial connection and a letting-go of past hurts and expectations. In other words, this is the first of the novels discussed in this book that both recognizes the validity of rebellion *and* posits that moving past rebellion to the reconstitution of the family unit, however changed, is possible.

Silence lies heavily over the relationships between all of the members of the Sai family. The novel starts with the death by heart attack of their absentee patriarch, Kweku. A gifted surgeon who abandoned his family and returned to Ghana after the loss of his prestigious position as the result of his expendability as a Black man to his employers, he succumbs to death, resigned, in the garden of the home he had designed to house a family that would only see it after he is gone. In *Body Counts*, Yến Lê Espiritu points out that "as complex and subtle as spoken language, silence, as a language of family, can protect and cherish and/or deny and control" (147). The truth of this claim is very evident in Selasi's novel, as both the parents and the children of the Sai family use silence as both a shield and a weapon. In the end, some things must be spoken, while others can be left in silence. A core aspect of the Sai children's reconciliation with their family unit is navigating what falls into which category.

Most of the first third of the novel follows the perspective of Kweku, the father whose cowardly choices negatively impact the lives of the rest of the characters. By first giving us Kweku's voice, offering us insight into his decision-making and even more crucially his insecurities, the novel forestalls a fully unsympathetic reading of his character even as it presents the fallout of his actions. At the same time, the novel does not suggest that his children can or even ought to develop the same level of sympathy for Kweku as might be produced in readers. His children's fraught relationship with their father is represented as entirely justified. This tension is made most explicit in the novel when Ling, the wife of the eldest son, Olu, tells him of his father, "Maybe it was the best he could do.... Maybe what he did was the best he could do" (306). It is significant both that this statement is said but also that it is said by someone who is not a blood member of the family. *Ghana Must Go* and, indeed, many second-generation texts, enact a reaching across generations both within the text and through the writing of the text itself. By attempting to enter the mind of and speak in the voice of members of the first generation, Selasi and other second-generation writers seek a kind of understanding that, as the narratives of the texts themselves demonstrate, is hard to come by within actual families. Key to the novel's approach is the idea that everyone's personality, behavior, and actions have sources and reasons behind them, however consciously or unconsciously, but that it is vital not to equate these things with excuses or explanations.

Rebellion, even in its more masochistic forms, is a fundamentally hopeful activity, insofar as it is predicated on the possibility for change, either in the self or the other. The novel explores this aspect of rebellion through Kweku's reflection on the women in his life as "dreamer-women" (48). In the process of contrasting "the women he's loved" with his new, simpler wife Ama, he thinks of his mother; his first wife, Fola; and his daughters as "doers and thinkers and lovers and seekers and givers, but dreamers, most dangerously of all" (48). In other words, these women are active and engaged, qualities he clearly appreciates about them. The danger he identifies is that these same qualities make them hopeful: "Very dangerous women. Who looked at the world through their wide dreamer-eyes and saw it not as it was, 'brutal, senseless,' etc., but worse, as it might be or might yet become" (48). This ability to imagine the world otherwise is dangerous for Kweku because it leads to these women being "insatiable" and "un-pleasable" not just with the world but with him. But this lack of satiability is not about seeing him as being inadequate; rather, what he fears is that they see him as being able to be more than he is able to see in himself: "And worse: who looked at him and saw what he might yet become. More beautiful than he believes he could possibly be" (49). Kweku is unable to live with this belief in him because it makes him feel his failures so acutely. Hope cannot exist without the possibility of disappointment, and Kweku cannot bear to be a disappointment. Moreover, he cannot bear to see disappointment in those he loves. That, after all, is the reason that he left: he could not bring himself to face what he believed would be his family's complete disillusionment with him, their realization once and for all that he is not A Success. In a way, Kweku is diagnosing the women he loves with cruel optimism, as defined by Lauren Berlant. As she points out, optimism becomes cruel when "the object that draws your attachment actively impedes the aim that brought you to it initially" (1). If the object of their attachment is Kweku as he could be and they were brought to it out of love for Kweku as he is, the object impedes the aim because their wish to see him be better actually pushes him to be worse. Ama, by contrast, "doesn't hurt herself. It doesn't occur to her" (49). Ama does not ask or strive for what she cannot have, and as a result, does not push Kweku away by imagining a better version of him; this, then, is the most meaningful difference between Ama and Kweku's two daughters. Taiwo and Sadie regularly hurt themselves. And this self-inflicted pain is rooted in hope.

The novel, which at various points follows closely the thought process and inner world of each of the family members, offers insight into the explicit choice to maintain silence on the part of immigrants. Fola contemplates the things that she never even shared with her estranged and now dead husband, Kweku, much less with her children, as she drives to the airport in Ghana to receive them. Reflecting on her university days, she thinks,

> Then, it seemed normal to lie there beside him alive in the present and dead to the past with the man in her bed, in her heart, in her body but not in her memory and she not in his. It was almost as if they had taken some oath—not just they, their whole circle at Lincoln those years, clever grandsons of servants, bright fugitive immigrants—an oath to uphold their shared right to stay silent (so *not* to stay the prior selves, the broken, battered, embarrassed selves who lived in stories and died in silence). An oath between sufferers. *But also between lovers?* (197)

This thought process reveals within itself its own cracks: they expect their silence to protect them from dying in silence. Their right to stay silent, to die to the past, ensures their fugitive state, as their oath requires them to curtail the intimacy they might otherwise forge with each other and with future children. This is particularly borne out through the parallels between Kweku's father's abandonment of his family and Kweku's eventual abandonment of his own as well.

Through the stories of both Kweku's and Kweku's father's undoing, Selasi draws attention to the coloniality of the US space and culture that often goes unmarked. The US is not only colonial in its relation to Indigenous people; its social structures are also based on the same hierarchies of race and class inherent in colonial social structures, which affect all who live there. Kweku desires to transcend the history that shapes him, to "have somehow unhooked his little story from the larger ones, the stories of Country and of Poverty and of War that had swallowed up the stories of the people around him and spat them up faceless, nameless Villagers, cogs" (91). This, for him, is the promise of immigration: "He didn't add it all up—loss of sister, late mother, absent father, scourge of colonialism, birth into poverty and all that. . . . He very simply considered it, where he came from, what he'd come through, who he was, and concluded that it was forgettable, all" (28). But that which he desired to forget and therefore to avoid grieving nevertheless stays with him. Kweku's father was "an artist, they told him, a Fante, a wanderer, a 'genius like him,'" who had, we are told in a parenthetical clause, "been jailed after punching a drunk English sergeant who'd hassled his wife, jailed, then publicly flogged" (58–59). Afterward, he left: "Just packed up his things, walked away, as he'd come. Others, now dead, claim he walked into the ocean in a sparkling white *bubu*, to his waist, then his head, without stopping. Further, forward, under, into the ocean. Like Jesus. With weights. Under the moon. Into black" (59). This story, presented tersely, nevertheless contains much of the rest of the novel within it. The mythical telling of his departure, through the use of the white traditional clothing and the comparison to Jesus, represents his departure as noble. Yet the abandonment that it elides means the struggle and poverty of the same woman that he was initially humiliated for defending. Kweku's mother, whose husband "abandoned her, more likely, unable to face her for shame" (60), must carry the burdens that his pride made him too cowardly to shoulder.

Decades later, Kweku makes the same decision his father once made, creating a cycle of paternal abandonment. Kweku is wrongfully dismissed from his job after he is pressured into performing a too-late surgery on the blue-blooded matriarch of an old-money Boston family, "Jane 'Ginny' Cabot—patron of research sciences, socialite, wife, mother, grandmother, alcoholic, and friend" (74). When the surgery is a failure, the hospital dismisses him to appease the dead woman's family. This ignoble and abrupt end to the life that he'd planned for himself and his family is beyond his ability to deal with, and he silently fakes going to work for months while he tries to fight the decision with his lawyer. When it is finally clear that he cannot win and when his secret is accidentally revealed to his son Kehinde as he watches his father being thrown out of the hospital that he once worked at, he leaves just as abruptly as his own father did. Like his father, his dignity is sacrificed to appease the ego of upper-class white people, and like his father, he cannot bring himself to face his wife when his humiliation is complete. When he speaks to Fola, he tells her almost nothing: "He said very simply that he was sorry and he was leaving. That if she sold the house at value, she'd have enough to start again. That it was quite possible that he had never actually deserved her, not really. That he'd wiped them out trying to beat the odds" (86). The silences between them remain in their parting. He sends "all his love to the children" (86), but this is not represented as quoted speech, as if to indicate that it is almost like saying nothing at all. This decision is the catalyst to all the family's undoing. And until his children go to Ghana to bury him, they know nothing of the story of his father. Kweku's silence about his own father might be intended to protect his children, but its actual result is that they do not have the tools to understand his behavior toward them.

After all, the belief that immigrant parents are able to truly hide the effects of their past from their children is a fallacy. They may be able to hide the events, but the ways in which those events have shaped them and their lives are visible despite their best efforts. Olu, the firstborn son, contemplates this issue explicitly: "He knew, though they hid it, that his parents had suffered, perhaps were still suffering in some unseen way; that it lightened their burden to think that their children would not suffer—and yet here he was" (221). The children's awareness of their parents' suffering is made all the more difficult to navigate because of the silence that shrouds it. Olu feels the responsibility to lighten his parents' load, but because he cannot know what that load consists of because they will not tell him, he must simply carry on doing what he believes will help them, which requires him to pretend not to suffer or struggle in front of them. The silence that is meant to protect the Sai children is actually damaging, precisely because it blocks the possibility for vulnerability and therefore intimacy that might help them to navigate a world that is not as different from the one their parents grew up in as their parents want to believe. The silence also prevents the children from seeing that their parents too are affected by a harsh and often racist world, an understanding that could be used to foster overt intergenerational solidarity rather than silence.

Like the novels previously explored in this volume, *Ghana Must Go* parallels the injustices of colonialism with the injustices of American racism to demand that the reader see the connection and reject American exceptionalism. Like it was for his father, Kweku's shame at the hands of white supremacy, his expendability in the eyes of those in power, is insurmountable for him. He reproduces the trauma he experienced despite having been so sure that he would not. But the novel does not frame this as inevitable—the empathy at the core of how he is represented is not absolution. The novel makes clear that, however bizarrely, it is a kind of male privilege to give up and leave. Women, after all, are also subject to the indignities and injustices of racism and colonialism but they must stay, must raise their children, must keep going. Of course, Fola does also engage in a kind of leaving by sending the twins to Lagos, based on very similar emotions to the ones that motivate Kweku's leaving. She too believes herself to be not good enough to guide her children. In the climactic confrontation during which Taiwo finally tells her mother of the abuse she and Kehinde experienced at the hands of Fola's half-brother in Lagos, Fola tearfully articulates her sense of inadequacy in the face of raising her children:

> I wanted you to have, I don't know, to have more. . . . Than a single mother. Than a mother like me. I didn't know what I was doing. I never had a mother. I was making it up as I went. I was scared. I was lonely. I was a coward. I was afraid of disappointing you, of holding you back from the things you deserved. You were gifted, so brilliant. Even smarter than Olu. Your teachers all said it. "She's special," they said. "Make sure to challenge her, stimulate, encourage her." I feared I'd be the reason that you didn't excel. I was afraid that I'd fail you. So I sent you to . . . him . . . and he hurt you. And Kehinde. I failed anyhow. (291)

In this moment, Fola is confessing the kind of vulnerability that mothers are not expected to show. Her self-recrimination is rooted in her own unprocessed losses, of her mother, whose death shaped her childhood, and of her educational goals, which she sacrificed in order to support her husband's career, having told him, "one dream's enough for the both of us" (73). Her vision for what her children deserved was built upon the classic foundations of immigrant striving that this book has engaged with throughout, the pursuit of the respectability that Susana Morris explores and the justification for past choices that erin Khuê Ninh addresses. Morris astutely points out that "respectability, at least as imagined through the current manifestation of the politics of respectability, is largely out of reach for many Blacks, which makes being judged by or internalizing a rubric informed by these politics unfair at best and cruel at worst" (3). Fola's position as a suddenly single mother is the result of a cascade of events over which she had no control—her husband's termination as a result of his perceived expendability due to his race and status as an African immigrant, his inability to face the reality of his situation or to share the burden of it with her, and his resultant abandonment of the family—yet she feels shame for these events happening to her. She has internalized the blame for her self-described failure by attributing it to not having a mother herself, rather than recognizing that the conditions surrounding the dissolution of her immigrant dream life were precipitated by external inequities.

Of course, Kweku, too, has carried out this same process of internalization by punishing himself and his family for the loss of his job and, as a result, the crumbling of his identity as a successful immigrant who has achieved the social mobility required of him to justify his place within the United States. Tellingly, when he was younger, Kweku believed that he would become worthy of Fola's love "not by having succeeded but by *being* a success" (73). Success in this formulation is an identity, not an activity. Fola and Kweku have internalized model-minority discourse so that they self-identify as a failed "production unit" (Ninh 2) within the US capitalist context. By judging themselves through this lens, they neglect to offer their children other forms of care that they can still provide without being conventionally successful and that are less capitalist in orientation. Fola's belief that the economic care of her children, meant to be achieved through sending them to Femi, was more important than their emotional care is what creates the circumstances of Taiwo and Kehinde's suffering. When she claims that they deserved "more," her understanding of what constitutes more is imaginatively constrained by notions of respectability and model-minority achievement. In this way, Fola does also, for a time, leave two of her children by sending them away. But because she is now the only parent, she must live with the consequences of this leaving when the children return, traumatized and changed.

It would be a mistake to read the application of respectability and model-minority ideology on the family unit as proof of a lack of profound parental love. Both Kweku and Fola love their children deeply; what they struggle with is the demonstration, the externalization, of this love, because to show it is to demonstrate a kind of vulnerability that neither parent is comfortable revealing. A partial consequence of the lack of vulnerability that Fola demonstrated to her children prior to their trauma is Taiwo's irrational but genuinely felt belief that her mother must have known what would happen when she sent them to Femi. In this same confrontation, Taiwo sobs, "How could you send us there? How could you send us? You knew what would happen. You knew, Mom. You knew" (290). By withholding the truth of what happened to them from Fola for all of the intervening years, Taiwo both protected and punished her mother and herself. By this, I mean that she protected her mother from the heartbreak and self-reproach that she experiences when she finally hears the truth, while also punishing her mother by forcing an impassable distance between them through silence, the silence that she learned from her parents' own practice.

This learned silence created a perpetual barrier between mother and daughter. Fola wants to connect with her daughter, "so longing to hold her, to squeeze out this *why*—and the sorrow and fury and shadow out with it, to hold her so tightly it all rushes forth, leaving breath bubbling out as when Taiwo was one and still longed to be held, and by *her*. But she can't" (238). The silence between them makes it impossible for Fola to reach for her. At the same time, her silence protects her from having to ever know for sure what her mother did or did not know, and it is a means by which she punishes herself by denying herself the comfort and intimacy that would help her heal. Her withholding forces her mother to pay attention to her, to continue to ask what happened. When they return, Fola begs them to tell her, but they refuse (238). This practice of withholding to keep attention, to force people to show that they care by chasing after her, is present in her relationship with her mother and with her eventual lover, the dean. Indeed, this is also one of the shared tactics that she and Sadie both utilize; Sadie's desire for someone to physically come look for her mirrors Taiwo's desire for someone to reach for her emotionally.

The abusive Lagos-based uncle Femi's home and lifestyle is a prime example of the postcolonial mimicry of colonial practices, as he both resents and idolizes his father's mixed-race first wife and models his household after a decadent colonial home, with uniformed servants and gaudy fixtures. The twins are sent away as a result of their parents' silences, and they respond to the abuse with a silence of their own: when they are returned abruptly to their mother, thanks to a chance encounter with an old friend of hers, they are changed but will not reveal what happened to them. They have learned the lesson of silence too well. They cannot bring themselves to speak their trauma, and their silence functions as a weapon on the part of Taiwo, the defiant former good girl, and as a bid at protection as well as the covering of his own shame for the peacemaker Kehinde, so their silence festers between the two of them, and between them and their mother, until the climactic moment of the novel when Taiwo reveals the whole story to Fola. Until this point, the source of their trauma had functioned as the text's central mystery, and its revelation both to Fola and readers serves as the ultimate moment in the text in which breaking silence allows for reconnection and the start to healing. Crucially, this form of verbal revelation is not the only way that healing begins in the story; there is a significant bodily element in the stories of Olu and Sadie, but most significantly through the text's subtle magical realism: Kehinde is able to participate in the moment of vulnerability and release between his mother and sister through the mysterious internal connection he shares with his twin sister.

The bond between the twins is rooted in the cosmology of Fola's people. The Yoruba belief that twins have certain mystical characteristics is taken up in the novel in interesting ways beyond the scope of this book, but relevant to the point at hand is that they lost the ability to hear each other in their heads because of the trauma they experienced, even though they continued to be able to feel each other's pain. After Taiwo has broken the silence with their mother, Kehinde is tentatively able to once again hear his sister's thoughts. The novel describes him as hearing "three words in silence, in the space between beds, her own voice in his head as he once used to hear" (308). These three words are never explicitly stated in the text, and Kehinde even doubts that he may have heard them, but their silent expression nevertheless triggers the beginning of healing in their relationship. The three words are implied to be "I forgive you," and Taiwo also "hears" these words in her head, coming from her brother (309); this mutual silent forgiveness is one of the moments in the text that identifies silence as not always a negative practice.

Kweku and Fola are both ruled by fear in a way that is passed down to their children unconsciously and which can only be overcome through a brave and dangerous turn toward vulnerability and an acknowledgment of the undercurrents that shape their lives in very real ways despite going unnamed. Kweku, strangely, experiences this overcoming through allowing his own death,[1] while Fola moves toward it through the breaking of silences with her children, both on her end and on theirs. The novel does not suggest that silence has no place, but it does demand a thoughtful consideration of how speaking, as well as listening to what is spoken and unspoken, is a fundamental part of working through the past and turning toward the future.

Thus far, this chapter has been primarily concerned with the roles of Kweku and Fola in their children's lives, in order to set the stage for how Taiwo and Sadie have internalized their parents' survival tactics, particularly their silence. Their incomplete understanding of their parents' pasts, coupled with the way that their second-generation positionality comes with often unspoken but acutely felt expectations, leads them to rebel in ways that are often self-destructive, as I have claimed. Through these self-destructive acts of rebellion,

---

1. The novel implies that, as a doctor, Kweku should have noticed the signs of the heart attack that kills him and that he essentially chooses not to make moves to save himself.

both women try and fail to escape their bodies and their social positions. In this way, Selasi is able to explore the figure of the rebellious daughter through two different characters, whose belief in their own difference from each other is undercut by the ways that their respective rebellions mirror each other in surprising ways. Despite Sadie's belief that they are "mismatched siblings" (150), the two sisters instead embody different versions of masochistic rebellion stemming from a shared source. Ultimately, both women are able to begin to heal through developing a better understanding of precisely what it is that they are rebelling against. This creates the possibility that they could reorient their energy in directions more likely to produce stronger physical and psychological connections to others and happiness within themselves. The novel's closing is hopeful but not conclusive to this end.

Taiwo's rebellion is more readily understood as such by readers and other characters within the story. But the actual contours of her rebellion are more complex than they might first appear to either set of observers. The desire to throw off the overwhelming weight of parental and social expectations is shared by most if not all rebellious daughters, but Taiwo's specific approach to fulfilling this desire is shaped by the particular ways that she conceptualizes what she is rebelling against and, just as importantly, what her rebellion means. As is often the case in stories following rebellious daughters, there is another, more dutiful child against whom the rebellious one contrasts herself. For Taiwo, this is Olu. She sees him as having fully embraced a model-minority life with his Taiwanese American partner, Ling: "What would he know about shame, Perfect Olu, . . . his girlfriend, their cold-white apartment, white smiles on the walls, *Ling-and-Olu do good in warm weather,* two robots, degree-getting, grant-winning, good-doing androids, a picture of perfection, New Immigrant Perfection, of cowardice rewarded" (127).[2] From Taiwo's vantage point, Olu has completely achieved the perfectly respectable immigrant dream life that they were all raised to pursue, and she scorns him for it. The emphasis on whiteness in this passage speaks to the assimilationist element of this vision of American success as well as to the sterility and purity associated with it. Her description makes clear that she believes that in order to live this life, one has to become an automaton. Significantly, Taiwo recognizes that her reflections on her brother are a self-defense mechanism; she acknowledges

2. Christopher T. Fan argues that Selasi's novel's depiction of the interaction between Asian Americans and continental African Americans demonstrates the convergence of the model minority and the flexible citizen. He argues of Olu and Ling that "their futures are mutually determined: Afropolitan identity offers a template for Asian American futurity, and vice-versa" (76). While this book does not take up flexible citizenship, because my focus is on the less flexible aspects of settlement in the US, this connection is worth noting.

her thinking as "an old habit, this, a bad one, to attack her attackers or whomever she perceives to be planning attack, right or wrong, noting all of their flaws in her mind, in this manner discrediting them" (127). Taiwo is very critical of what she sees as Olu's concern about external judgment: "Olu's five-minute speech about Sai family glory, what Others Must Think of Them, *oh the shame*" (127). Yet the only means by which she is able to escape the same preoccupation is to convince herself that the person judging her is flawed; she cannot justify her own actions to herself, so she must reject the judger rather than the judgment.

Nonetheless, one of the most important interventions of the rebellious daughter is the recognition that the perfect immigrant family picture is fundamentally a performance. As Taiwo speculates on what Olu will say to her on the phone when she initially avoids his call, she imagines that he "might call her a 'failure' for withdrawing from law school, condemn her as 'reckless,' 'disappointment to Mom,' the final blow to the production, *Successful Family* in shambles, curtains closed, theatre shuttered forever" (128). Taiwo understands the family as a theater troupe that has suffered some setbacks as a result of their father's abandonment, making her fall from model-minority grace via an illicit affair that precipitated her withdrawal from law school a confirmation that the troupe cannot continue to put on the show titled *Successful Family*, cannot maintain the shared enterprise of performing immigrant acceptability. Olu's internalization and application of expectations are, readers know from the sections of the text focused on his perspective, rooted in his own complex relationship with their father and his actions. Since my focus here is just on the Sai daughters, though, it is most pertinent to pay attention to how Taiwo perceives Olu, more so than exploring Olu's self-perception. From her vantage point, he is completely removed from the circumstances that govern her behavior: "How can he know what it is to be stared at and talked about; worse, not to care, to give in to it? He who knows nothing of hot things, of wrong things, of loss, failure, passion, lust, sorrow, or love?" (128). Significantly, Taiwo conflates not caring about what others think with giving in to their perceptions of her here, two actions that could be read as different from each other. To give in suggests more than just disregarding the opinions of others; to give in is to lean into those judgments, to accept them as true. This is what makes Taiwo's rebellion distinctive: she is not disagreeing with what should be but rather letting herself be consumed by what she agrees should not be. The use of the word *consumed* is purposeful here, as Taiwo herself thinks of her behavior in terms of consumption: "the ravenous urge to be swallowed, digested, to pass through a body only to drag oneself back to the mouth of the beast" (128). This grotesque image sounds torturous both for the beast and for the one being consumed. It also suggests a deeply *against* sensibility: the desire to be both close and abject.

Crucially, Taiwo's rebellion does not free her from performance. As I pointed out at the beginning of this chapter, Taiwo sees herself as an overachiever only performing a bad girl, sexpot persona. This alternative persona can be read as a waystation before her full transformation into a rebellious daughter because she is still fulfilling some of the expectations placed upon her through her academic achievement. It is just as much a performance as the "Darling Daughter. The brightest of pupils, who never looked out, who had spent half her life with her head in a book, learning Latin roots, spewing right answers" (128). The capitalization of "Darling Daughter" identifies it as a role, and the ensuing characteristics make clear that what makes her the dutiful and therefore darling daughter is her academic performance and her self-contained behavior. Her rebellion, then, does not lead to a truer self but rather another performance, particularly because she is rejecting what is expected of her but without embracing anything in particular. She has some idea of what she is running from, but very little idea of what she is running to, much like the other rebellious daughter protagonists previously explored in this book.

A core aspect of Taiwo's characterization is her physical beauty. Her striking appearance shapes her experience of the world. She resents it and sees it as a constant barrier between herself and the rest of the world: "Her efforts to make or keep friends came to naught: there was always the issue of beauty between them, as envy in women, desire in men, indistinguishable in the end, lust and envy, co-original, the flower and leaf of the same twisted root" (128). While this interpretation might seem vain in a novel where she was the only character whose perspective is represented, the rest of the novel bears out that Taiwo's beauty is a fact and not a delusion. This beauty is both unasked-for gift and unasked-for curse, tied to her greatest trauma but also something that she cannot resist using to her benefit. The degree to which she curates her appearance is especially reinforced when she discusses her hair: "Dreadlocks are black white-girl hair. A Black Power solution to a Bluest Eye problem: the desire to have long, swinging, ponytail hair" (138). Here, she references Toni Morrison's classic debut novel to highlight the role of internalized white supremacy in Black beauty practices, even those associated with Afrocentricity. Indeed, *Ghana Must Go* explicitly connects dreadlocks with a specific kind of respectability when Taiwo claims that the kind of Black girl who grows locs, outside of Rastafarians, are "Black girls who go to predominantly white colleges" (138). This is a strong example of the ways in which respectability practices are not always fully legible to those they are meant to appease. As Taiwo both resents and leans into cultivating her physical beauty, it becomes clear that she sees it as an element of her fate, another aspect of her life that gives her a sense of lacking agency even in those instances when she is making choices.

The novel represents Taiwo's affair with Dean Rudd as both self-destructive rebellion and genuine romance, refusing a clichéd reading of a highly overdetermined set of circumstances. Before the narrative of their meeting is even described, the novel depicts the public reaction to their affair, stating that "when the press learned, they made it sound natural: a tale old as time, beauty, power, and sex, dean of law school in love tryst with editor of Law Review, BEAUTY AND THE DEAN! in 'Page Six,' and the rest" (128–29). This sensationalized reading of the affair is contested, not because it is wholly false but because it is a massive oversimplification that is most interested in detailing the "Golden Boy['s]" fall from grace. While "it was natural, that it happened, that Girl in a city that adulates blondes should find Boy (fifty-two, former blond turned to silver-and-gold) in a city that adulates youth" (129), Taiwo and Dean Rudd, and their relationship with each other, are represented as far more complex than the sensationalist reading allows.

The novel asserts the instant attraction between Dean Rudd and Taiwo at their first meeting. Her self-presentation is described in detail:

> In blue velvet blazer and dress-cum-dashiki, the tongue-in-cheek dress code, half devil-may-care, quarter Yoruba priestess, quarter prim British schoolgirl, her upsweep of locks dripping tendrils, high heels, with that feeling of conquest she still sometimes gets before entering rooms in which points must be won, in which men must be smiled at and women impressed, prey and predator both. (130)

This passage emphasizes both her sense of herself as performing as well as her recognition that she is navigating others' power while simultaneously exerting her own. Taiwo is aware of how people perceive her because of her beauty and can use it to her advantage but has never truly thought of it as her own: "with the body, as always, a stranger post-coitus, the long, lanky limbs and congenital tone, a good body, she'd heard, though she didn't believe it, or couldn't quite see it, not least after sex" (136). Taiwo's estrangement from her own body makes her fall for Dean Rudd even more unlikely and therefore even more dangerous to her well-being.

Taiwo cries over the "crushing disbelief in the truth of their love" (137). However much their love is rooted in projection, in the desire for youth or the desire for power, their love was real to the lovers. This decision to sympathetically portray both Taiwo and Dean Rudd (the narrative refers to him with his title even during their intimate moments [136]) while also acknowledging the reality that their affair is not outside of social relations allows the narrative to explore the tension between appearance and reality. Taiwo is an active participant in the affair, but she does not reveal it on purpose; instead, the novel suggests that it is a passive sort of carelessness on her part that allows the relationship to be discovered. It might be easy, then, not to read the affair as rebellion at all, since it was not meant to be uncovered. But I read the recklessness that allowed them to be seen by a friend of the dean's wife as representative of masochistic rebellion because it is an example of Taiwo putting herself in harm's way. In her discussion of self-destruction and rebellious Asian daughters, Ninh argues that this behavior entails a "deferral of accountability" and that "self-destruction incriminates, because it implies causality and responsibility on someone else's part" (117). Ninh's focus in this section is on suicide, and while Taiwo does not try to kill herself (though her twin does attempt suicide for reasons connected to their shared trauma), she does commit a form of social suicide in that she makes it impossible for her to return to what she is leaving behind; having this affair come to light means the end of her reputation as well as of her law career before it even started.

Taiwo articulates this deferral of accountability explicitly: "She wasn't particularly angry—at least not with her lover; she'd been angry with her lot now for fifteen odd years—but she wanted him to suffer, and not from disgrace, but from a sense of having failed her. Of having caused her to fail" (206). This perverse desire for his pain is an echo of her general desire to remove the expectations placed upon her—"her lot"—without having to be the cause of the removal. She imagines herself as having an audience whose judgment she is actively pursuing: "So that all of them, seeing her failure, would puzzle, would ask in hushed tones how this girl, this success—summa cum laude, NYU! PPE, Magdalen College! summer associate, Wachtell!—came to fall on her sword, whereon the answer would come if not to them who were asking, then to him: *Because he let her*" (207). Like her parents, she has internalized a model-minority vision of success, but rather than strive for it and fail, she wants to opt out while having someone else to blame for it. Or, rather, more than just someone: "There was the other one, the first one they'd deleted, the one who had backed down a sunset-lit drive while she watched from the window obscured by darkness" (207). This passage makes it clear that Taiwo is displacing her resentment toward her father onto her older lover. His foundational failure creates the conditions for her failure, and she longs to force him to confront this. She seems to believe that she will gain something meaningful through his pain, perhaps because "the infliction of grief is less unfortunate by-product than naïve logical inversion: one must protect the family to be filial; one must harm the family to be free" (Ninh 152). Taiwo's desire to be free of her own pain but also of external expectations requires her to do harm.

Poetically, Taiwo's practice of imagining her life as a movie is inherited from her father, and she uses that same practice to fantasize about confronting him with her failure: "He'd see her from the driveway and slow to a stop with that look on his face per that scene in such films when a man on the run returns before dark and the hit man is waiting, at ease, in plain sight, with his boots on the railing, a gun in one boot where the man in the driveway can see it" (207–8). The image of her as an assassin is significant; she believes that she will be doling out a punishment by confronting him. But the punishment is, again, masochistic, as what she imagines herself revealing is her own living death: "He'd see in her face that a light had gone out and would know without words that his daughter was dead, that the girl he had left on a street in North America was not the one sitting on this stoop in West Africa, with boots propped on railing and pistol in boots, that she'd died because no one would save her" (208). Her death, her failure, would be a recrimination of him, not her.

In this way, Selasi adds another layer to the debtor/creditor relationship between immigrant parent and child identified by Ninh (16). What happens, after all, when the creditor fails to provide that which the debtor is expected to pay back? By deserting his family, Kweku effectively abdicated his position as creditor, leaving his children with a debt to an absent figure. Each of his children react to this severed relationship of exchange differently; Olu, for example, still strives to make his father proud, to pay his debt, despite the absence of his father to receive these offerings. He is, in a sense, constantly trying to transfer deposits into a closed account. Taiwo, by contrast, longs to repay his failure to provide through demonstrating her failure to deliver. She wants to force him to reopen the account, for the sole purpose of demanding he acknowledge its emptiness. This desire to compel him to confront that "he'd been too weak to protect her" (208) hints at the way that she conflates her experience of sexual trauma produced by Uncle Femi with her failure to stay on the path of immigrant upward mobility. After all, her imaginary confrontation with her father is precipitated by her leaving law school in disgrace, yet the actual revelation she wants him to experience is to have to face her spiritual death as a result of her uncle's abuse and her subsequent inability to talk about it with anyone. Importantly, Taiwo's rebellion is not entirely framed as being directed toward her parents as people so much as against her role in the family and in the world. She is aware that her parents are not the authors of the script that orders their lives; she sees them struggling with it even as she herself does. So, her anger toward them is at times more about their failure to shield her from these unfair metrics of success than anything else. Because she cannot wholly direct her fury toward her parents, Taiwo is unable to fully direct her rebellion outward.

Taiwo's masochistic rebellion comes from this problem of direction; she is able to rebel against her role but not to choose a role she truly wants to inhabit. Indeed, by embracing an image of herself as a temptress, she is acting out a role that was cruelly projected onto her at a formative stage in her life. The abuse that the novel finally reveals near its end is even worse than a reader might have guessed because it involves forced complicity. By making Kehinde engage in incestuous acts under threat of having someone else molest Taiwo, Uncle Femi ensures that the twins are both closer and farther away from each other because they now share a shameful secret that has ruined the innocence of their love for each other. The way that this experience sexualizes Taiwo at a stage when she was only beginning to understand herself as a sexual being—she has just begun masturbating when this trauma takes place—contextualizes her uncomfortable relationship with her body and sex as well as her strained relationship with Kehinde. When she goes to talk to him about her "scandal," she tries to get him to tell her what he thinks. Though he initially resists, her prodding leads him to say something almost unforgivable, supplying the word "whore" as she lists ways that he could describe how she had behaved (177). Their subsequent confrontation brings what has been bubbling under the surface to the forefront as Kehinde claims, "It's not your fault, Taiwo. It's my fault. You know that—" to which Taiwo replies, "Is that what you think? It's your fault I'm a whore?" (178). Both Taiwo and Kehinde are caught within their own self-reproach, but Kehinde's is especially powerful because he seems to believe that everything that goes wrong in Taiwo's life is his fault. Taiwo has tried to direct the anger she feels toward her closest sibling and confidante elsewhere to preserve their relationship, but this confrontation between them makes this redirection no longer possible. While Kehinde is also a victim of their uncle's twisted actions and therefore cannot bear full responsibility for what he was made to do, Taiwo has the right to be angry and hurt, and their silence around their shared trauma has only made it fester and has increased their inability to understand each other's feelings about it. The fracturing of this particular relationship is difficult but necessary for the twins to be able to reform their relationship on firmer ground.

In contrast to Taiwo's more overt role as rebel, her youngest sister, Sadie, understands herself as a good girl who by nature plays second fiddle to more glamorous and more rebellious women like her sister and her best friend and crush, Philae. Her self-perception as "dutiful, fair-to-middling if affable. The wind beneath. The other the bird" (150) may be superficially true, but her inner life is ruled by a self-directed masochistic rebellion that is arguably even more damaging than that of Taiwo. After all, Taiwo sacrifices her reputation and her relationships, but Sadie sacrifices her body. Like Taiwo, Sadie's behavior is rooted in a misdirection of her anger as a result of a lack of knowledge and context. The presence of both sisters in the novel, then, offers two separate images of self-harming rebellion. The silence that plagues the intergenerational relationships in the novel is manifested once again in Sadie's often inept performance of it.

By virtue of birth order, Sadie is the farthest removed from her parents' past. All of the children are born in the US, but Sadie is born after the family has achieved the immigrant dream and is fully entrenched in a largely white upper-middle-class world. The novel signals her distance explicitly through a childhood anecdote. Sadie finds Fola's only Kente cloth throw while playing dress-up. She wraps herself in it and announces to her mother, "I'm a Yoruba queeeen!" (153). Of course, Kente cloth comes from the Akan in present-day Ghana; she is wrong about both nation and state. This level of ignorance of her own heritage is notably not rectified by her mother, as Fola, struck by the emotional resonances of the throw, only responds by tearily telling Sadie that she is "a little princess" and then "never said more, never speaks of her past" (153). In Fola's desire not to burden her daughter with the past, she refuses to give her the resources to craft an identity that is not defined primarily by whiteness.

Sadie's position makes her the ideal Sai to explore what it looks like to have only absence to pin an identity to. From her perspective, *model minority* is her only real culture. This is conveyed when she describes her understanding and experience of race. Framed as a response to the regular accusation from Taiwo that Sadie "secretly wants to be white," Sadie draws a meaningful distinction between white and what she refers to as a "patina of whiteness, or WASP-ness more so" (146). Rather than accepting that she specifically is not authentically Black, a concept that she argues "confuses identity with musical preference" in a parenthetical clause, she asserts that she is part of a larger class category: "Be they Black, Latin, Asian, they're Ivy League strivers, they all start their comments with overdrawn ums, they'll all end up working in law firms or hospitals or consultancies or banks having majored in art. They are ethnically heterogeneous and culturally homogenous, per force of exposure, osmosis, adolescence" (146). Like her other nonwhite, cultural capital–acquiring peers, her sense of self is far more about what she is trying to be as opposed to what she is already, perfectly in keeping with Ninh's characterization of model-minority identity. Yet while Sadie claims that she "accepts this without anguish as the price of admission" (146), she is always acutely aware of her outsiderness. She is, as Homi Bhabha would say, "not quite / not white" (131). Indeed, she is most comfortable, paradoxically, where she knows she is not meant to belong (158). Sadie has fully internalized her position as striving outsider who knows that she will never be completely let in.

Under these conditions, perhaps it would seem strange to describe Sadie as a rebel. Yet she is the tragic combination of model minority and rebel, as her performance of good girlness facilitates her socially unacceptable acts. Take, for example, her obsession with her friends' bathrooms. Sadie is always invited over to her friends' houses because she is perceived as a "Good Influence" by her friends' parents (143), which gives her access to their most intimate spaces. There she snoops, indulges in small acts of "clumsy kleptomania" (143), and, most tellingly, wipes her hands on the family's bath towels. None of these acts are individually that terrible or that unusual, but their combination, compulsiveness, and location mark them as of a piece with her major rebellious act, her bulimia. The towel-touching especially signals a desire to impose herself on others, to assert that she is real and present and has an effect, but without those she is imposing herself on actually knowing. Its secretiveness is part of its masochistic nature insofar as it provides her a small pleasure (getting one over on people) and a larger pain (fear of getting caught, guilt at doing something she knows she is not supposed to) without gaining any true benefits. At the same time, the bathroom is a haven because it is one place where she does not have to perform. She finds lying fully dressed in the bathtub appealing when she is "exhausted from making an effort" (144). The performance of the good influence, the sweet and clever friend, "so bright, and so nice, and so *cute,* like a member of the family" (144), is tiring because, like all acting, it requires large amounts of energy to achieve. This element of performance is, of course, a core aspect of the model-minority identity she has so fully embraced. The wording of the aforementioned performance is significant here because it combines patronizing language meant to be imagined in the mouths of rich white parents with the all-important phrase "like a member of the family," which, as I explored in my analysis of *Brown Girl, Brownstones,* is a rhetorical strategy of the wealthy that claims intimacy while maintaining difference through the important distinction housed in the word *like.*

Her bathroom activities are made possible precisely because she is so liked and underestimated by her peers' families. The stakes are higher in relation to her eating disorder. Her bulimia not only hurts her physically, but it also requires meticulous work to cover up. Here she applies her classic model-minority skills—thoroughness, observation, unobtrusiveness—to maintain secrecy. She carefully cleans both herself and the bathroom, making sure to use Handi Wipes on the floor because "sometimes the person who uses the bathroom next notices, if she doesn't attend to the floor" (142). This practice is part of what makes her purging a ritual, a "gruesome rite" (142). It is a sacrifice to an unappeasable god that is only truly successful if it is not detected. The push and pull between the desire to be unseen and the desire to be sought and found is a natural result of the threat of both hypervisibility and hyperinvisibility. To be seen can mean being identified as different, but to be totally overlooked is also a sign of difference, as it signifies a lack of identifiable humanity and a lack of belonging. In Sadie's role as Philae's sidekick, she is able to negotiate this position by casting herself as the narrator, who is always the friend (145). The friend of the protagonist has some degree of power in her role as the storyteller; she is able to control how much she is or is not seen.

My analysis of Sadie's eating disorder builds on previous scholarship that has also identified her bulimia as a form of rebellion. In comparing the novel with Tsitsi Dangarembga's classic novel *Nervous Conditions,* Aretha Phiri identifies Sadie's bulimia as expressing "'a covert but disruptive act of rebellion' (Hill, 1995: 87) against an entrenched (Western) heteronormative sociocultural imperialism" (151). She goes on to argue that "in this way, that which is most personal/domestic, that to which she is so intimately attached—the body—becomes, in Sadie's act of purging, a complicated, political vehicle against, and ironically embodied expression of, an historical *and* contemporary limited cultural imagination" (Phiri 152). Phiri's analysis demonstrates the dual direction of Sadie's againstness; by bingeing and purging, she is constantly vacillating between moving toward and away from white Western beauty standards, toward and away from the disciplined body, toward and away from wanting to be seen and to remain unnoticed and, as a result, unchallenged.

Sadie's sense of her own invisibility is a misreading of her family's coping mechanisms even as she engages in the same ones; she too practices silence by hiding her feelings and her activities but does not quite understand that her mother or siblings' lack of commentary about her bulimia and her sexuality is also an exercise in silence. The narrative makes clear that both her eating disorder and her unrequited romantic love for Philae have not escaped the family's notice. In thinking about her own body, Taiwo notes that she "had inherited and maintained with no effort the model-esque figure that Sadie so craved" but also blames Sadie's body issues on their mother: "Fola, who, frightened by the baby's low birth weight, had overfed Sadie and babied her sick" (136). Taiwo is again here reflecting on herself as acted upon rather than as an actor; she did not choose her body. Taiwo goes on to think, "The disorder. Unmentioned. Though all of them saw it. If only she could, she'd have said, 'Sadie, here, take my body, I don't want it. I never even liked it. It's not like I asked for it'" (136). Taiwo does not, however, feel that she can say this to her sister. The use of the phrase "asked for it" is especially resonant here, as this thought process comes on the heels of a discussion of Taiwo's own disordered relationship with sex, during which she makes specific mention of "the Thing That Happened in Lagos" (136). The discourse of "asking for it" in situations of rape or sexual assault relies on the idea that victims are responsible for their own victimization, a belief that should of course be roundly rejected. Interestingly, here, Taiwo is mobilizing the phrase to refer not to what has happened to her body but to her body itself. Taiwo, thus, feels violated by her own body. One possible reading of this sense of violation is that her traumatic sexual experience happened at the unwilling hands of her twin, whose body she felt was part of her own until Uncle Femi rewrote their closeness as abominable. The masochistic rebellion that Taiwo enacts is rooted in this antagonistic relationship with her body. Here, again, the two sisters have more in common than they acknowledge; they both hate their bodies and maintain silence around that hatred yet continue to act in ways that both inadvertently reveal that hatred and that silently plead for the people they care about to notice.

The desire to be noticed by loved ones but the refusal to ask for this attention is core to Sadie's character. She describes a "game that she plays with herself, or against" (144). The use of the word "against" here is significant because it is an acknowledgment that in this game, every win is a loss and every loss is a win since she is essentially betting against herself. The goal of the game is to "guess how many seconds it will take them to notice that someone's gone missing, that Sadie's not there" (144). This "game," such as it is, originates with her family, but she also plays it with her friends, especially Philae. As a child, Sadie hoped that it would be Taiwo who came to find her, not Olu; Sadie's desire to be seen by her sister particularly mirrors Taiwo's relationship with their mother. At the moment that Sadie's game is introduced in the novel, her absence has already been noted, as she is being called to the phone. Because no one specifically comes to find her, however, it does not count as being found. In other words, the offer to come to someone does not fulfill the desire to be chased after. When Taiwo finally does come to find her, it overpowers all other thought and feeling: "She'll hear only her voice in her head in the quiet *she came she came she came she came she came*" (160). This moment of connection is not the resolution of the sisters' mutual resentments, but it does signal the novel's investment in the role of breaking old patterns to move toward better futures.

Through Fola and Sadie's relationship, this novel masterfully depicts the way that closeness and distance can coexist. Despite Taiwo's jealousy at her sister and mother's intimacy, Sadie too feels the performativity and the silences in their mother-daughter dynamic. In contrasting Fola to Philae's mother, the narrative describes her reaction to her children's emotions: "Whenever one of them shouts at her she simply tips her head and waits. It's not exactly patience, nor dismissal, something in between, an interest in the shouter's plight, an empathy, with distance" (156). This distance is perhaps what makes it possible for Sadie, the child closest to her mother, to feel like the family is unreal. She tells Fola, "we're not a family" (156). Fola tries to both correct her daughter and skim over the hard feelings that this comment is obviously rooted in by saying, "I can assure you, you all came from me," but her subsequently calling Sadie "baby"—which the whole family does regularly—precipitates a seemingly long-overdue outburst from Sadie. Sadie's tearful insistence that she is "NOT A FUCKING BABY ANYMORE!" and that she is "nineteen—practically twenty—years old" (156) reads as a bit childish but also as a genuine reaction to the strain of haunting silence present in the endless weekends and holidays they spent, just the two of them.

This confrontation signals Sadie's first externally directed act of rebellion, of refusing to leave unsaid what is usually silenced in their relationship. At first it does not seem successful; Fola reacts by telling her, "Go live your life" and hiding in the bathroom for hours (157). Here, Fola makes use of Sadie's usual sanctuary to separate herself from her daughter. But this willful breaking of the silence between them leads to meaningful changes in the lives of both mother and daughter that ultimately contribute to the hopeful ending of the novel. Fola abruptly moves to Ghana soon afterward, giving Sadie the space she claimed to want. This space is painful, but it also forces Sadie to confront her reality: "She cries very softly for all that *is* true, for the loss of that man and for missing her mother, how light things became and how lost she's become, how alone they all are, how apart, how diffuse" (158). The idea that the family is "light" is mentioned several times in Sadie's section. While *light* often has positive connotations, in this context it emphatically does not; a light family is a rootless family, one that does not leave a mark, that can be blown away by the wind.

While Sadie's outburst toward Fola is a first important step in her growth within the novel, the primary resolution of her masochistic rebellion must take place internally. Some have critiqued the resolution of Sadie's narrative as cliché and reliant on an essentialist idea of belonging (Phiri 157). But I think these critiques underemphasize an important aspect of her growth. Sadie's primary trouble is that she feels as though she has no family and no history, and as a result she cannot contextualize herself or, importantly, her body in a way that imbues her with value. Her desire not to be seen comes from the fact that she has not experienced being seen well. When the family goes to see Kweku's family in his ancestral village, she is prepared to go on being unseen.

She stands in "the broken doll position she perfected in high school, with shoulders hunched forward and flip-flops turned inward, an arrangement of limbs that conveys such unease that the onlooker invariably feels uneasy himself and after one or two seconds looks away" (264). This bodily discomfort is rooted in being in a world where she was not valued and not recognized—her white, affluent high school.

What breaks her out of this instinctive practice made to "throw off the would-be observer" is twofold: encountering someone who refuses to look away and finding in that someone a "striking resemblance" (264). Her aunt Naa reflects her back to herself and does so without being deterred by Sadie's posturing. Significantly, this moment of recognition sparks thoughts of self-hatred. Simply seeing her face in another's does not make her appreciate her own. She asserts that "she isn't pretty" as a matter of fact (264). She compares herself to her sister and mother, as she has all her life, and argues that they cannot understand her because they are pretty, that "their empathy is bound within the limits of their reality" (265). Of course, the same is true of Sadie; her disdain for her aunt and by extension herself is also constrained by the extremely limited corner of the world that she has been exposed to thus far. Her inability to see this in herself is what prevents her from moving beyond the surface-level understanding of her self-perception that "accepts that the media are to blame for her bulimia, her quiet, abiding desire to be reborn a blond waif" (265). Her imagination is limited because before this point, she had no real proof that another worldview, another mode of evaluation, was possible.

Sadie's lack of imagination is particularly evident in her belief that Shormeh, the girl asked to entertain these honored guests by dancing, "doesn't have the look of a dancer" (267). She notes immediately that Shormeh's body is like her own, and so her feeling of pity and disgust toward the girl is an expression of her self-hatred. By seeing herself from the outside, she is forced to confront how she feels about herself: "It startles her to think this so clearly of another, so cruelly, of this dancer, but the thought comes again. *I hate this body*, she thinks and she stares at the girl, *I hate this body, it is ugly, I hate how it looks*" (267–68). While recognition is often associated with comfort, seeing herself in another finally makes Sadie genuinely acknowledge her self-loathing and her belief that "the body is the reason she cannot be seen" (268). This idea can be read in two ways: that the body is what prevents her from being seen, but also that the body is the justification for her to rightfully not be seen. Both interpretations suggest that the body itself is intrinsically flawed. This moment of honesty, though, of breaking silence within herself, is what makes her able to begin the process of transcending these limiting beliefs.

It is not some essential, primordial Africanness that changes things; it is a connection to a specific family, a specific past, and a specific form of bodily movement that offers her a different lens through which to view her own body than she has had before. The familial element is emphasized by the physical resemblance as well as Shormeh's insistently referring to Sadie as "*sees*-tah" (267). Indeed, more than her surprising facility with the dance, it is the moment of being hailed, of being seen and engaged, that is most profound for her: "No one will know what it is in this moment that overwhelms Sadie, not even Sadie herself, as the insistent lead dancer catches hold of her elbow and repeats, tugging gently, 'Please *sees*-tah, please come'" (269). In this moment, it is as if she has shown herself kindness and confidence through the conduit of Shormeh. Sadie is not only doing something she believed was not for her, she is doing so in a place and in a way that reorients her understanding of the thing itself. Her body knows what to do because this is her cultural patrimony, but also because for once she trusts it, allows herself to be fully in it, to not see herself from the outside: "unaware of the exterior, unaware of the skin, unaware of the eyes, unaware of the onlookers" (270). Sadie's self-perception throughout the novel can be usefully viewed through the lens of double consciousness as theorized by W. E. B. Du Bois in the way that she is constantly described as seeing herself through the eyes of her white peers.

Double consciousness is complicated for immigrants because it is a mode of seeing that they encounter after having lived otherwise. Of course, Black immigrants coming from the Caribbean and formerly colonized African countries are not untouched by white supremacy, but the experience of being a part of a racial majority creates different conditions of experiencing and engaging with it. For the second generation, they are born into the world that produces double consciousness, so their experience more fully resembles what Du Bois describes as arising from specific experiences of racial alienation, while being raised by parents whose experience is different from their own. Sadie's life is deeply shaped by her sense of double consciousness, and this dance might be read as her first glimpse beyond the veil, not into white America, which she knows intimately but is always only precariously a part of, but into a version of herself seen from within.

The masochistic rebellion that this chapter has explored is, in Sadie's case, rooted in rootlessness. By encountering her body in a different context, by seeing what it can do when unconstrained by Western standards of beauty and movement, Sadie begins to see differently and to see what it can mean to be truly seen. At the end of the novel, her narrative is not tied into a tidy bow—the narrative does not depict the end of her bulimia, which would have been an offensively facile resolution to a major medical and psychological condition. But the embrace she shares with Fola after the dance, the renewed connection to her family overall, and her truthfulness within herself at least suggest a move toward intimacy and honesty hitherto absent from her life. The open-ended nature of her story arch is not only appropriate because of her youth—recall that she is a first-year college student at this point—it is a necessary acknowledgment that one transcendent experience does not undo a lifetime of saturation in American white supremacy.

While the intragenerational conflict in Selasi's novel is not wholly unique amongst the texts explored in this book, its attention to cross- and same-gender sibling relationships is notable. The connection between Taiwo's and Sadie's rebellion and resolution is more explicitly explored than the sibling relationship in *Brown Girl, Brownstone*, for example. In practical terms, writing a novel that meaningfully engages with multiple siblings is difficult on the level of creating a coherent and not overly long narrative. Each of the Sai children do not necessarily get equal billing in *Ghana Must Go*, but each of their stories add to the novel's exploration of second-generationness, particularly in the way that it demonstrates the variety of relationships they can have with the previous generation. The contrast between Sadie's relationship with their mother and Taiwo's prevents a totalizing reading of mother-daughter relationships in Black immigrant literature, demonstrating that intergenerational conflict can look different ways even within the same family. As with my analysis of Sadie's revelation, I argue that this is a part of the novel's insistent specificity, despite its engagement with common themes and tropes.

It is significant that Taiwo's confrontation with her mother is precipitated by her reaction to Sadie's moment of transcendence, in keeping with the theme of reading and misreading at the core of their relationship. Taiwo is upset to see Fola hug Sadie in this "moment of triumph" (270) because, she thinks, "If only I was easier, then I'd be hugged too" (271). Her belief that she is difficult and therefore unlovable is easy to translate into anger at her sister because she associates these conditions to each of their designated (if unspoken) roles in the family: "This is her preassigned part of the family play, as it's Olu's to administrate or Kehinde's to peacekeep or Sadie's to cry at the drop of a hat or their mother's to turn a blind eye: Taiwo sulks. They expect it, await it, would miss it if she stopped" (271). Despite her rebellions, she still feels locked into a distinct place in the family's dramatis personae. That is, here still she is playing a role, just as she was as Dutiful Daughter and as temptress. The narrative makes clear how overly simplified Taiwo's casting of her siblings is, contributing to the narrative's picture of a familial system that works for no one but which everyone feels forced to carry on enacting. This depiction is important because it demonstrates the way that immigrant family dynamics of the kind the Sai family embodies are in fact a system that goes beyond individual relationships; their position as a "production unit" (Ninh 2) dictates the limits of their behavior. In the context of the novel, production has a key double meaning: it is both a production in the manufacturing sense and the theatrical sense. The family performs for the world and for each other in order to produce the product that is a successful immigrant family.

The novel makes it clear that just as Sadie's invisibility is both externally imposed and self-inflicted, so too is Taiwo's unapproachability. She feels "rage and self-pity and shame at self-pity" (272), a mix of emotions that is rooted in punishing herself for feeling things she believes she should not feel. Thus, while Sadie's reconciliation must necessarily happen within herself, Taiwo's must be enacted externally with Fola—it requires honesty, revelation, and, crucially, overt anger. Not just brooding but direct and unpleasant expression. As unusual as it might seem, the antidote to Taiwo's unhappiness is the willful conclusion of her rebellion through finally telling her mother the truth. Only by making herself truly abject in her own estimation does she become huggable in the way that she has longed for:

> Fola lurches forward, catching Taiwo as she buckles, managing to grab her by the shoulders as she slumps to the sand. The movement is instinctive—less embrace than intervention—but it puts their skin in contact for the first time in years. Taiwo jerks backwards, the dizziness mounting. She tries to say "Don't" and erupts in tears. (290)

Even at this moment, Taiwo is struggling against the contact she has most longed for. In the embrace, the two women are finally honest with each other, and just as importantly, they both recognize what Fola can actually do for Taiwo, now, so long after she was traumatized: "All she can do is stand weeping with Taiwo alone on this beach in the bearing down heat, knowing someone has damaged her children irreparably, unable to fix it. Able only to hold" (291). Taiwo has been denying herself this much longed-for touch through her refusal to be honest with her mother. She has been pulling against her desire to be against her mother, skin to skin, and in this context her againstness has not served her well. One could argue, of course, that it should not be Taiwo's responsibility to reconcile with her mother, but by not doing so, she was punishing herself just as much as she was punishing her mother. The masochistic nature of her rebellion means that regardless of how valid her grievance, the means by which she manages it limits her ability to live well.

As I mentioned above during my analysis of Fola's reaction to Taiwo's silence, crucial to Taiwo's resentment toward her mother is the belief that her mother should have been aware that Femi was bad and that bad things would happen to Taiwo and Kehinde in his care. This belief is based on the idea that Fola "must have known somehow what would happen, who he was, her own brother, her own family" (274). Yet while Taiwo asserts that you must know your own family, the novel fundamentally rejects this idea. Indeed, the degree to which you might not know your own family is a central aspect of the narrative, as each relationship between siblings as well as between parents and children is full of misreading, misunderstanding, and miscommunication. Taiwo envies Sadie, Sadie envies Taiwo, both Taiwo and Kehinde feel that they need the other's forgiveness, Fola thinks that Taiwo does not want to be close to her, and Taiwo thinks that Fola does not love her the same way that she loves Sadie; these are only some of the ways in which the members of the Sai family fail to know each other. This lack of mutual understanding is connected to their feeling of rootlessness, to the parental silences that ground the family in unsteady terrain, and to the near inevitable immigrant and second-generation difference in experience that can only be overcome if it is actually acknowledged with empathy on both sides. This turn toward empathy is signaled through Taiwo finally speaking to her mother and hearing what her mother has to say, and the mutual forgiveness that the twins silently communicate to each other.

The novel signals that moving forward is possible through the tentative forms of reconciliation with each other and within themselves that each of the characters go through toward its end. Significantly, the turn toward the future is suggested through recognition of the humanity and limitations of the parents, especially Fola, as she is still alive. At the very end of the novel, Fola has an imaginary conversation with Kweku by talking to a drawing of his face in the dirt done by Kehinde. In this conversation, she reconciles with him and admits that he was not the only one between the two of them who left the other. She identifies this as connected to their shared immigrant experience: "We were immigrants. Immigrants leave" (316). This statement is definitionally true—but this novel, like many other immigrant and second-generation novels, is just as interested in the numerous resonances of this leaving beyond the fact of moving from one country to another.[3] Fola calls herself and Kweku cowards and imagines Kweku replying, "*We were lovers,*" to which she replies, "We were lovers, too" (317). They were both, and one does not negate the other. This exchange also explicitly raises a question that has been bubbling under the surface throughout the narrative; Fola imagines

---

3. Notably, Fola also returns to Africa, not to her native Nigeria but to Ghana. This immigrant permanent return is underdiscussed but increasingly common, as I explore in the next chapter.

Kweku asking, "*Couldn't we have learned? Not to leave?*" (317). Tellingly, the novel refuses to answer this question directly. Selasi is a second-generation writer who, in writing this scene, is imaginatively reaching across generational lines. The question of whether the first generation could have been different or done better is perhaps not for her to answer even if it may be for her to ask. Rather than answer this question, then, Fola thinks about her own limitations: "One can learn only so much in one life" (317). As I argued earlier, the performance and pretense of invulnerability was part of what damaged her relationship with her children in the first place. This coming to see the limits of her abilities, then, is actually more honest and therefore opens up the possibility of a greater intimacy with her children than what was available when she refused to open herself up. Her final response to the imaginary Kweku is vitally important to the novel's overall representation of the intergenerational context it depicts; she states, "we learned how to love. Let them learn how to stay" (317). Immigrants leave, but the second generation must decide what to do with the aftereffects of their arrival and, as this novel suggests, their departure. A part of this, the novel suggests, is learning to stay.

The rebellious daughters at the heart of this novel need to learn how to stay in order to stop inflicting masochistic rebellion upon themselves. They must learn to stay in several ways: stay with themselves, stay with their bodies, stay with their loved ones, stay with their pain as well as their pleasure. As both women have learned, the escapes that they make for themselves through bingeing and purging, through an illicit affair, through hiding or leaving in hopes that someone will try to come and find them, cannot free them from what they actually want to leave behind, because these forms of escape are in actuality repetitions of that which hurts them. This is not to say that either the novel or I suggest that they should become Filial African Daughters, as Taiwo would put it, but rather that they must seek a place for themselves in their own future and amongst their family that is not reactive but instead imbued with agency. The path of being the perfect model minority is not available to either of them—Sadie's queer journey is only just beginning, and Taiwo is still no longer in law school and must find a way forward for herself beyond the classic immigrant daughter playbook. I argue, then, that reconciliation within the family unit is not incompatible with continued and, indeed, more productive rebellion against social expectations of immigrants' daughters. By turning the rebellious instinct outward rather than inward, these women may be moving into a future less controlled by the pains of their parents' and their own pasts and more dictated by a clear-eyed rejection of the constraints placed upon them and a greater opportunity to consider what they actually want.

CHAPTER 4

Rebelling against Stereotypes and Confinement

The protagonist of Chimamanda Ngozi Adichie's 2013 novel, *Americanah*, writes in a blog post, "Americans assume that everyone will get their tribalism. But it takes a while to figure it out" (186). In this entry of Ifemelu's blog, which is interspersed throughout the narrative, she describes American social and racial politics in a way that purposefully imitates the way that American media discusses the rest of the world. By using the term *tribalism*, she defamiliarizes that which American readers likely take for granted and explicitly names the entrenched hierarchies and antagonisms of American society that are considered impolite to discuss out loud, particularly the "ladder of racial hierarchy in America" in which "white is always at the top, specifically White Anglo-Saxon Protestant," while "American Black is always at the bottom, and what's in the middle depends on time and place" (186). Adichie's novel places Ifemelu as an observer of American society even as she experiences and is changed by it. In so doing, she engages with the intersections of race, class, gender, and migration through a personal lens by rooting her representation of the gender-inflected racialization of Black immigrants in the life of a young Nigerian woman who migrates while still in the process of coming of age.

The preceding chapters of this book have focused on novels that follow second-generation daughters, raised in the US by immigrant parents. This novel, by contrast, is about a daughter who herself immigrates without her parents. *Americanah* follows Ifemelu from her childhood through her teen years in Nigeria, to her migration to the United States and her life there, through to her eventual decision to move back to Nigeria and establish herself there for the long term. This core difference sets *Americanah* apart from the other texts, but its inclusion here is important because it offers the opportunity to consider how the dynamics of racialization, gender formation, and place-making that are explored in second-generation contexts overlap with as well as differ for immigrants who arrive while on the cusp of adulthood. Like the other protagonists that this book has explores, Ifemelu is affected by American racial and gendered hierarchies and expectations, but she does have firsthand, formative experience of another political and cultural context that has its own rules and structures, which she experienced at an age where she could process it consciously. Like the other protagonists, she experiences intergenerational conflict and misunderstanding, but she does so from afar for most of the novel. Significantly, despite being meaningfully transformed by life in the US, Ifemelu moves back to Nigeria. This aspect of the novel signals a shift in the trajectory of the imaginative possibilities for Black immigrant daughters in US fiction. Narratives of permanent return were comparatively uncommon in twentieth century Black immigrant novels and, indeed, immigrant novels more broadly. When returning to the ancestral homeland long-term does take place, it is often in an involuntary context, such as deportation or children being sent unwillingly by their parents. As such, there has been limited scholarship about immigrant return narratives. The idea that a permanent return to the ancestral homeland is a genuine possibility was not present in either of the twentieth-century novels I've discussed in this book. In *Brown Girl, Brownstones*, the idea is presented as pure and potentially dangerous fantasy, and in *Breath, Eyes, Memory*, return visits are necessary and transformative but the possibility of returning to stay is never seriously considered. Part of this is the result of the specific historical and geographical contexts those novels represent, of course; midcentury, still-colonial Barbados and dictator-ravaged Haiti are understandably represented as difficult sites of return even in novels that explicitly critique life in the US. In *Ghana Must Go*, traveling to Ghana is important and life-changing for the second-generation characters, and the novel ends while they are all still there, but there is no indication that they are likely to stay, though their mother has moved there for good. In other words, the novel does suggest the idea that a first-generation character's return can be portrayed as a good and, in their own life, progressive move, which differs from the twentieth-century portrayals. A specific set of national and economic circumstances in Nigeria and Ghana in the early twenty-first century makes the possibility of permanent return more common in real life and more representable in fiction, and this undoubtedly plays a significant role in *Americanah*. However, the protagonist's Nigerian upbringing is also an important part of what separates Ifemelu from her second-generation American counterparts, whose ambivalent positioning in the US nevertheless solidifies it as their home.

In this chapter, I focus specifically on the novel's metatextual elements, particularly the protagonist's writing within the text, to explore how this aspect of the novel makes explicit the dynamics that served as powerful undercurrents in the previously explored novels. By focusing on how the protagonist, Ifemelu, narrates her own burgeoning and intersectional understanding of race in America, oftentimes in defiance of a variety of conventional viewpoints both within the US and in Africa, this chapter argues that Adichie's novel exemplifies a form of againstness rooted in the tension between what it means to observe the world and what it means to live in it. Ifemelu's writing is how she makes sense of her own experiences, but as she does this through an anonymous blog and, eventually, other forms of public writing, she translates these experiences into assertions about the world that make meaning as much as they reflect events. This meaning-making enterprise is an act of rebellion, as it interrogates and at times resists the reification and naturalization of American ideas about race while simultaneously acknowledging the role these ideas play in her life, thus refusing the role of the African immigrant model-minority subject, whose "success" eliminates the effects of race and racism. Crucially, Ifemelu's blog posts reflect her own changing ideas about race, gender, the body, and other concerns and are at times critiqued within the narrative of the novel, making it inappropriate to read her blog as simply the mouthpiece of the author. But Ifemelu expresses herself, even when the text suggests that she is wrong, and this emphasis on the inherent value of her expression is itself a core aspect of this novel.

The use of a blog as a metatextual device in the text, wholly appropriate for its mid- to late 2000s setting, serves to ground the novel in its time as well as to offer a secondary means by which to represent the protagonist's engagement with the world around her. This was, after all, the era during which blogs, short for weblogs, became a powerful form of communication and, in many ways, transformed public discourse. Much writing about blogs at the time reads now as overly optimistic, to say the least, but it is important not to underestimate how impactful the lower barrier for entry to having a public platform was for many. Indeed, although the term *blog* did not make it into the dictionary until 2005, by "2008, an estimated 133 million blogs had been created, and approximately 120,000 new blogs are started each day" (Davis 4). That a great many of these blogs originated from the US was possible because "by 2008, according to the Pew Internet and American Life Project, 73 percent of Americans were online" (Davis 4). This is in stark contrast to the statistics about the African continent; in 2007 only 3.6 percent of people in Africa had access to the internet (Somolu 477). Thus, Ifemelu's placement in the US is a significant aspect of not just the content of her blog but the possibility of its existence.

The participation of African women in this newly developing space was, therefore, both rare and powerful. Writing around the same time that the novel takes place, Oreoluwa Somolu asserts the empowering potential of blogging for African women:

> It appears that the power of the blog as a tool for empowering women lies in its ability to provide an avenue for women to express themselves and connect with other women. The ability to write anonymously is regarded as an important factor in enabling women to share their experiences and opinions honestly and openly. Since, as one blogger puts it, women can be "very truthful and open about things we wouldn't dare talk about in public," women can be encouraged by and learn from each other. Many women capitalise on the ability of blogs to be "a powerful conversational tool with the potential to reach a wide audience" and to "empower by giving a voice to the unheard." Through "story sharing, encouragement, education, and words," women "promote strong positive images." (483)

Somolu's assertions are reflected in Ifemelu's blog and the comments it receives, as her anonymity for much of the blog's run gives her a freedom that she does not feel when speaking publicly (307), and the readers' comments referenced in the texts often reflect the sentiment of giving voice to the unheard, such as the response to her post about depression (160). Of course, Ifemelu also fits the profile of the African woman blogger that Somolu identifies, by being highly educated (482), which tempers any reading of either the fictional Ifemelu or her real-life counterparts as subalterns. Even though Ifemelu struggles economically and socially during her time in the US, the novel does not deny that her cultural capital and education shape her self-understanding and give her certain kinds of access.

While all who theorize about the nature and the effect of blogs argue that they lower the barrier for entry for amateur and average people to contribute to and potentially lead public conversations, some have critiqued the idea that blogs produce a totally new form of political discourse. Davis argues that "political blogs affect politics through a transactional relationship with other agenda seekers (politicians, groups, political organizations, etc.), journalists, and the audience. This thesis is significant because it contradicts the conventional wisdom that blogs represent both a distinction from and a reform of the existing communications and political systems" (7). Instead, he argues, "not only have political players adapted to the blogosphere, but the blogosphere has in turn been mainstreamed in order to acquire relationships with other players" (8). Davis is primarily concerned with what one might call "big *P*" political blogs, that is to say, those involved in party politics, whereas Ifemelu's blog is often focused on "small *p*" politics, meaning discussions about the politics of everyday life, including issues related to race, gender, and class, although the novel also includes four entries specifically about Barack Obama, Michelle Obama, and Barack's presidential campaign (215, 299, 322, 338). Davis's assertion that blogs become intertwined with preexisting structures and institutions is borne out by the way that Ifemelu's success as a blogger leads her to become a speaker on the "diversity talk" circuit (306). Despite her own feeling that she is unqualified and her apprehension that people who ask to interview her or invite her to speak will "realize that she was play-acting this professional, this negotiator of terms" (306), her integration into the corporate and educational landscape of "diversity workshops" (307) is built on the success of her blog, thus legitimizing the blog, which in turn leads to more speaking engagements, creating a self-sustaining cycle.

Significantly, what she says in her workshops and what she writes in her blog are quite different; in her workshops she "began to say what they wanted to hear, none of which she would ever write on her blog, because she knew that the people who read her blog were not the same people who attended her diversity workshops" (307). The purpose of her blog is to create a community of interest and is skewed toward topics relevant to other people of African descent, both American-born and otherwise, but its offline result is a reputation for Ifemelu as a "'leading blogger' about race" (307), whose presence appeals to vaguely liberal, largely white institutions that ultimately want the credibility of bringing someone in to talk about "race" without the threat of being truly challenged. She learns that her in-person audiences are interested in the "gesture of her presence" rather than the "content of her ideas" when she first attempts to honestly express her ideas and receives a deeply underwhelming response (306–7). While she does not love giving these talks, it pays for her student intern and allows her to purchase a small condominium. The blog's transformation into economic enterprise leads her to feeling "subsumed by her blog" (308). Perhaps especially because of the dissonance between her blog and her talks, she fears her readership, imagining them as "a judgmental angry mob waiting for her, biding their time until they could attack her, unmask her" (308). The blog platform's leveling of the playing field is a double-edged sword; gaining fame through her writing creates the concurrent possibility of becoming infamous. Moreover, despite the fact that she asserts that she is not an expert (306), she is still received as such and tacitly agrees to being framed that way by accepting speaking gigs. What, after all, qualifies someone to be a "race expert" outside of the academic sphere? The stakes of eventually being wrong or making a mistake are thus always getting higher the longer she blogs.

Despite the eventual monetization and complication of the blog, its origin is reflective of the authenticity and hope associated with the genre at the time that the novel is set. The reader has already encountered several entries of *Raceteenth* before its genesis is revealed. Ifemelu's sense of her own racialization is dramatically increased by dating a rich white man, Curt, who is prone to overlooking or denying instances of racism that Ifemelu experiences when they are together. She notices that "there were, simply, times that he saw and times that he was unable to see" (296). The variability of this seeing is part of what frustrates her; if he never saw, it would be easier to understand. This tension culminates in an argument about the representation of Black women in print media; Curt describes the African American–focused *Essence* magazine as "racially skewed" (296), and Ifemelu responds by taking him to a bookstore to show how little representation of Black women there is in mainstream American magazines. Unsatisfied by Curt's placating rather than apologetic or appreciative response to her demonstration, Ifemelu goes home to write a long email about the cracks in her relationship to her Kenyan friend Wambui. Her friend responds by telling her, "This is so raw and true. More people should read this. You should start a blog" (298). This episode serves to set the stage for Ifemelu's feelings that she expresses in her writing, but it also works to remind readers of the media landscape that blogs emerged in opposition to. The rise of blogs focused on experiences and identities largely ignored in mainstream media was a core part of the genre's success, as readers hungry for representation that they had not otherwise encountered flocked to engage with content that made them feel seen. Even blogs without explicitly political intent could contribute to a conversation about representation by simply reminding the public that, say, Chicana women might also be interested in makeup (309). The novel's depiction of the power of blogs to amplify perspectives ignored by traditional publishing is tempered, however, by the reality that writing for public consumption does not necessarily free a person from their ingrained social conditioning.

Blogs were often born out of intimate dialogue and authentic emotion; nevertheless, the reality of audience shapes the genre significantly. While Somolu notes that among African women bloggers, "the ability to write anonymously is regarded as an important factor in enabling women to share their experiences and opinions honestly and openly" (483), Adichie demonstrates the difficulty of developing that level of honesty through Ifemelu's experience of posting her first blog entry. Once she breaks up with Curt, she uses the popular blog hosting platform WordPress to launch *Raceteenth or Curious Observations by a Non-American Black on the Subject of Blackness in America*. Her first post is "a better-punctuated version of the e-mail she had sent Wambui," but when she realizes that nine people had actually read it, she panics and takes it down, only to re-upload it with what must presumably be a much more palatable conclusion than the original. In it, she claims that "the simplest solution to the problem of race in America" is "real deep romantic love, the kind that twists you up and wrings you out and makes you breathe through the nostrils of your beloved" and then goes on to argue that segregation within American society prevents such love from emerging and, as a result, "the problem of race in America will never be solved" (298). There are a number of ways to read this strange claim. One reading is that Ifemelu is ultimately still naïve about the nature of race in America and about the nature of love and therefore genuinely believes this narrative, despite the ways in which the example of her own romantic relationship does not support this perspective. Another reading, based on the fact that she added this amendment when she realized she actually had an audience, is that it is a self-protective lie that she knowingly tells to make her story more palatable to the audience that she does not yet know. Or, more harshly, this conclusion can be read as a cynical display of false romanticism in order to endear herself to readers who might feel personally affirmed by the idea that their romantic relationship is revolutionary, actually. Whichever of these readings one chooses, what is clear is that the novel disavows Ifemelu's claim here.

This disavowal is demonstrated by the fact that the story is told in the context of a dinner party years later, during which she rejects her own previous position when she argues against a Haitian woman who claims that "she had dated a white man for three years in California and race was never an issue for them" (292). In this way, the novel charts Ifemelu's growth through her changing relationship to her own previous views. Ifemelu has to grow into the ability to write freely and authentically, and even then, what that means changes throughout her life. As an observer as well as experiencer of race in America, her reflections on it are shaped not just by what happens to her but how she has internalized what is expected of her.

It is notable that the first entry of the blog concerns romantic love and that this entry is introduced more than halfway through the narrative. Dating and relationships are incredibly popular topics of online discussion, of course. But beyond that, the fact that it is her interracial relationship that produces the crystallization of her racial consciousness is telling. As Carole Boyce Davies points out, "'Blackness' is a color-coded, politically-based term of marking and definition which only has meaning when questions of racial difference and, in particular, white supremacy are deployed" (7). The novel's representation of her undergraduate career makes it clear that this is the period during which she "becomes" Black in the sense that she describes in the blog post "To My Fellow Non-American Blacks: In America, You Are Black, Baby," which I will discuss in more detail shortly. Yet, during that time, she finds her place primarily with other African international students and is generally represented as being buffeted about by her racial experiences rather than being in a position to articulate them.

Her naivete is demonstrated by her uncritical reading of the ways in which Curt fetishizes her in their relationship: "Later, when he wanted to do impersonations—'How about you be Foxy Brown,' he said—she thought it endearing, his ability to act, to lose himself so completely in character, and she played along, humoring him, pleased by his pleasure, although it puzzled her that this could be so exciting for him" (197). Both Curt's whiteness and his wealth provide a sense of freedom for her: "With Curt, she became, in her mind, a woman free of knots and cares, a woman running in the rain with the taste of sun-warmed strawberries in her mouth" (198). This relationship transforms her life and subsumes her identity: "She was Curt's Girlfriend, a role she slipped into as into a favorite, flattering dress" (198). But this proximity to privilege, which affords her numerous advantages she would not have otherwise enjoyed, also leads her to understand herself as Black through the power of contrast with whiteness. In university, she came to understand herself as separate from African Americans through the division between the "American-African" and the "African-American," who were associated with the African Students Union and the Black Students Union respectively (141). In her relationship, she is able to recognize that this distinction is much less meaningful in the white, privileged world that Curt brings her into, where she would be the exotic Black girlfriend even if she were African American. This is signaled by Curt's desire for her to perform as Foxy Brown, which could be in reference to either the titular character of the 1974 blaxploitation classic or the rapper who took her name from the film. Both character and rapper are associated with specific visions of American Blackness (the rapper's Chinese, Indian, and African mixed Caribbean heritage notwithstanding). The closer to whiteness she comes, the more her Blackness becomes visible to her. This is not a critique of Ifemelu; like all immigrants, she is an amateur ethnographer. Her keen observation of the world around her is rooted in the need for self-preservation and self-fulfillment. Through her blog, Ifemelu moves from amateur to semiprofessional.

The promise of the model-minority position is that those who embody it gain functional equality with white people through economic success, even if they are still perceived as culturally foreign (Nguyen 146–47). This promise is dependent on the model minority's usefulness as a tool to shame other minorities, principally African Americans, for their lack of success by showing "what can be achieved through self-reliance rather than government assistance, self-sacrifice rather than self-interest, and quiet restraint rather than vocal complaint in the face of perceived or actual injustice" (Nguyen 147). As I have explained elsewhere, this is a devil's bargain that demands immigrants and their children accept their own social inferiority to white Americans in order to establish their social superiority over African Americans. The novel explicitly addresses these dynamics in a blog post in which Ifemelu writes that "American racial minorities—blacks, Hispanics, Asians, and Jews—all get shit from white folks, different kinds of shit but shit still. Each secretly believes that it gets the worst shit. So no, there is no United League of the Oppressed. However, all the others think they're better than blacks because, well, they're not black" (207). In other words, maintaining a position above Black people in the racial hierarchy serves as a form of compensation for non-Black minorities, even if they still experience and know themselves to experience oppression. Nevertheless, this is a bargain that many immigrants, including African immigrants, accept as the price of doing business in America.

In the novel, Aunty Uju represents this compromised approach, to disastrous results. Her insistence that her son Dike should not see himself as African American, coupled with her resistance to teaching him anything about his Nigerian heritage, leaves him without a sense of identity; as Ifemelu puts it to her aunt, "You told him what he wasn't but you didn't tell him what he was" (380). In the confrontation between Aunty Uju and Ifemelu after Dike's attempted suicide, Uju argues that she told her son, "You are not black" because she did not want him to "start behaving like these people and thinking that everything that happens to him is because he's black" (379–80). This argument is a classic example of model-minority discourse and is based on a refusal to see that while not everything that happens to him is because he is Black, he still needs the tools to understand those situations when what happens *is* a result of or reaction to his Blackness. The use of "these people" is especially deliberate, as it creates a strong sense of otherness toward those to whom it is applied, African Americans.

Ifemelu's in-between position, as a young immigrant who arrived on her own, gives her clearer eyes through which to view both other immigrants and their children. She is able to understand her cousin Dike's plight and can remember what Aunty Uju was like prior to her immigration transformation. In Nigeria, Uju was playful, ambitious, and not overly concerned with morality, as she was the mistress to "the General," a member of the military government (45). In the US, Uju has taken on a new and more pious persona, and has embraced the "assimilationist, individualist, upwardly mobile professional class" identity that erin Khuê Ninh writes about in the Asian American context (11). She is still ambitious but the form it takes has changed in order to conform to her new context, especially because she is a mother. Ifemelu's in-between perspective extends beyond her direct family; she comments on another couple of Nigerian immigrants whose sons she sees are "caged in the airlessness of their parents' immigrant aspirations" (218). The airlessness described here is a symptom of the debt-bound familial relationship that Ninh describes: "The construct of 'filial obligation' defines the parent-child relation as a debtor-creditor relation, but within the system without contract or consent, the parent-creditor brings into being a child-debtor who can never repay the debt of her own inception and rearing" (16). In this context, any parental request and demand is rooted in the debt, and therefore refusing to wear a specific shirt to church, as Dike does, is an act of ingratitude and rebellion rather than a simple act of personal preference. Ifemelu is discomforted by this dynamic, especially because she herself has been in some ways liberated from many forms of filial responsibility through her migration. Still, she is sympathetic to her aunt, whose anxieties she understands, "making her way in unfamiliar terrain as she was" (218). With no children of her own and having arrived young and relatively unencumbered to the US, Ifemelu's ability to mediate between her aunt and cousin comes from her position between their two generations. Aunty Uju's position as immigrant mother, on the other hand, makes her pursuit of a model-minority identity understandable even as it is represented negatively.

Other critics have noted how the novel foregrounds the structural positioning of African immigrants within the American racial field. Christopher T. Fan argues that "Ifemelu's outsider perspective (in the context of the United States) and its potential for honorary whiteness (a potential secured precisely by her critique of whiteness) renders her perspective structurally equivalent to that of Asian Americans" (79). While I do not agree that she is able to attain honorary whiteness beyond the incredibly limited circumstance of being physically present with Curt, his comparison to Asian American positionality is nonetheless apt.

In this context, the blog post "To My Fellow Non-American Blacks: In America, You Are Black, Baby" is an explicit rejection of model-minority logics. But this post is also written in a deeply ironic tone and in a deliberately scattered style that prevents it from being read as a straightforward statement of solidarity. Instead, this blog entry is just as much about resignation as it is about connection. The post opens by arguing that non-American Blacks only assert "I'm Jamaican or I'm Ghanaian" because "you know black is at the bottom of America's race ladder. And you want none of that" (222). She is not arguing that these identities do not matter but rather that "America doesn't care" (222). Here, she asserts that the desire among African and Caribbean immigrants to maintain distinction between themselves and African Americans is purely self-serving. She describes her "initiation into the Society of Former Negroes," an experience that she argues non-American Blacks all have, as a time in undergrad during which she was expected to give "the black perspective" despite having no idea what that was (222). The demand to speak for all Black people is, of course, also inappropriate when directed at African Americans, but it is even more divorced from reality when applied to a young African who has barely begun living in America.

Significantly, much of the remainder of the blog entry is tied to the state of confusion produced by this process of becoming Black in America. She identifies several things that non-American Blacks need to learn to do, most of which are about learning when to be offended and how not to be offensive. These examples highlight the specificity of US-based racism and purposefully defamiliarize it for the reader. The idea that liking watermelon—an incredibly popular fruit globally—is both associated with Blackness and has negative connotation is identified as absurd through Ifemelu's confusion about why her classmate asked if she did and her other classmate's reaction to the question. More potently, Ifemelu illustrates the incoherent way that Black women are perceived by pointing out that all Black women must be described as "STRONG" and then cautioning her women readers that they should not speak their minds "as [they] are used to doing in [their] country" because "in America, strong-minded black women are SCARY" (222–23). The distinction here between strong and strong-minded is key. Black women in America are expected to be strong in the sense highlighted by the famous passage from Zora Neale Hurston's *Their Eyes Were Watching God*: "De nigger woman is de mule uh de world" (36): they are expected to bear the weight of the world without complaint. Being strong-minded, on the other hand, involves asserting oneself, and such self-assertion, in America, can lead to a woman being demoted from "strong Black woman," a respectable category, to "angry Black woman," an object of fear and loathing. Ifemelu's distinction also works to undermine the common US understanding of itself as superior in the area of women's rights; Chandra Talpade Mohanty's argument that Western feminism produces discourses of Third World difference that "are predicated upon (and hence obviously bring into sharper focus) assumptions about Western women as secular, liberated, and having control over their own lives" (353) is echoed in Ifemelu's perspective. She also advises that "if you are a man, be hyper-mellow, never get too excited, or somebody will worry that you're about to pull a gun" (223), acknowledging the way that Black men are also gendered. These examples work to show how both African Americans and non-American Blacks are subjected to absurd racial logics that are made more visible for non-American Blacks because they have other experiences against which to contrast those they have in the US. Because in their home countries, their identities are formed around other affiliations that are experienced just as "naturally" as race is in the US, identity reformation for the non-American Black, as Ifemelu describes it, requires confronting a foreign, inexplicable new identity and learning to resign oneself to it.

The activities that come with accepting this new identity are listed in a way that foregrounds how decisively personal this process of reformation is. She asserts that part of becoming Black is learning to take responsibility for the actions and the well-being of other Black people, especially in relation to white people. The examples she gives are tellingly based on decidedly middle- to upper-class experiences: interacting with service people, attending an Ivy League college, tipping in restaurants (223). The non-American Black must compensate for the perceived failures of other Black people, and she must also resist the urge to set herself apart; she is not to argue for her presence in an elite institution from a personal standpoint, by whipping out her "perfect grades in high school," but rather she must "gently point out that the biggest beneficiaries of Affirmative Action are white women" (223). The imagined reader of Ifemelu's blog post is clearly a well-educated foreign-born person like herself, for whom a sense of solidarity with African Americans is often primarily formed by interacting with white Americans rather than through becoming embedded in African American community. This is particularly highlighted by the end of the post, which concludes with an explanation of how to tell a non-Black person when something racist happens to you. Ifemelu lists the rules of engagement as follows: "Make sure you are not bitter. Don't complain. Be forgiving. If possible, make it funny. Most of all, do not be angry. Black people are not supposed to be angry about racism. Otherwise you get no sympathy" (223). This advice is purposefully ironic in that its goal is more to point out the unfair nature of how Black people are expected to cope with racism than to actually recommend these behaviors. What is framed as a list of recommendations for Black people is revealed to be a critique of whiteness through the last few sentences: "This applies only for white liberals, by the way. Don't even bother telling a white conservative about anything racist that happened to you. Because the conservative will tell you that YOU are the real racist and your mouth will hang open in confusion" (223). The white liberal reader of this blog post might feel superior to the white conservative described but is likely to also feel called out by the description of their own fragility that precedes it.

The end result of Ifemelu's blog post, then, is a sense of Black immigrants as conscripts of American racial discourses whose only choice is to accept these discourses and learn to navigate them. They might want to decide for themselves how they feel about things, but this option is not available: "Even though you would like to be able to decide for yourself how offended to be, or whether to be offended at all, you must nevertheless be very offended" (223). Ifemelu is not unaware that African Americans are also subjected to a system not of their own making; the heart of the distinction between the subjects of her post and their African American counterparts is, in fact, the idea that there is an element of choice for the immigrant: "When you make the choice to come to America, you become black" (222). Coming to America is a choice, becoming Black is not, but both are inextricable from each other. Particularly among the middle- and upper-class immigrants that she pictures as her audience here, the unsteady nature of their privilege is one of its core attributes. There is no denying that they have access to certain kinds of privilege and, even in comparison to middle- and upper-class African Americans, a different relationship to identity, but their conscription into Blackness has the potential to neutralize this privilege in many situations, especially those involving white people. The non-American Black must still "stay well away from the crime area for weeks, or you might be stopped for fitting the profile" when a Black person commits a crime (223), must still argue with a Young Republican about affirmative action even if they were not a beneficiary of it, and must still be cognizant of racial stereotypes and refrain from behaving the way that they would have in their home country to avoid how that behavior might be read; in other words, they must still adhere to respectability politics and perform respectable Blackness despite their relative privilege. Brought closer to whiteness by their model-minority status, they are nevertheless subject to the demands of respectability, especially because of this proximity to whiteness, as it puts them into the position of being, however reluctantly they might accept it, a bridge between white people and African Americans.

The novel does not solely represent spaces where non-American Blacks associate with white people. Its main events, however, do take place primarily in spaces of privilege, including such spaces occupied by elite Black Americans. Ifemelu's next serious boyfriend is Blaine, an African American university professor, whom she describes as a having not a normal spine but a "firm reed of goodness" (311). Just as she did with Curt, Ifemelu throws herself into the world of her boyfriend even though she never feels fully comfortable within it. With Curt, she took on the trappings of wealth and freedom, while with Blaine she takes on the markers of respectable, Black middle-class behavior that is characterized by bodily control: "She began to floss, as she began to do other things that he did—going to the gym, eating more protein than carbohydrates—and she did them with a kind of grateful contentment, because they improved her. He was a salutary tonic; with him, she could only inhabit a higher level of goodness" (312). His influence in her life extends to her blog: "At first, thrilled by his interest, graced by his intelligence, she let him read her blog posts before she put them up. She did not ask for his edits, but slowly she began to make changes, to add and remove, because of what he said" (313). She does not let this stand for too long, however, and begins resisting his interventions, though not wholly successfully. When she tells him that she wants to observe, not explain, he argues that she has a "real responsibility" and that by not giving more depth to her posts, she is "being lazy" (313). As a paragon of respectability, Blaine demands that Ifemelu join him in his goodness both in their personal life and in her writing.

One meaningful contrast between Ifemelu's experience as a daughter who is an immigrant and the daughter of immigrants is the way that her parents' physical distance allows her freedom she would not have had otherwise. As the previous chapters have suggested, immigrant families might exercise even tighter control in the site of settlement than they would in the homeland to guard against the real and imagined threats of life in the West. For Ifemelu, she is able to live her life and respond to her parents more freely: "Ignoring [her father], even telling him that she was moving in with a man to whom she was not married, was something she could do only because she lived in America. Rules had shifted, fallen into the cracks and distance and foreignness" (315). Her foreignness is not, therefore, only a source of difficulty but also a source of liberty in the context of her familial relationship. Her parents' confusion at her decision to be in a relationship with "an American Negro" (315) is something that she can laugh at rather than allow it to influence her decisions.

Indeed, there is a certain freedom in her foreignness even within the US, revealed particularly through her relationship with Blaine. It is clear that Blaine has fully internalized the idea that he must be an example of appropriate Blackness and expects Ifemelu to play that role as well. So, when she allows an older white woman to touch her natural hair, he is upset with her, saying, "How could you let her do that?" (314). For Ifemelu, she sacrificed little to allow this woman the experience of touching a Black woman's natural hair, but from Blaine's perspective, she has set a bad precedent. Despite her adaptability, Ifemelu struggles to fully transform because she does not feel, on a fundamental level, what she "should" feel according to Blaine: "He expected her to feel what she did not know how to feel" (314). Blaine is not incorrect that in the context of the US, touching a Black woman's hair, even after having asked, is a textbook example of what have been termed racial microaggressions, which are defined as "brief and commonplace daily verbal, behavioral, or environmental indignities, whether intentional or unintentional, that communicate hostile, derogatory, or negative racial slights and insults toward people of color" (Sue et al. 271). The issue of hair-touching is so commonly known that it has been featured in BuzzFeed comedy videos and inspired the title for a song by popular R&B singer Solange, "Don't Touch My Hair." Yet Ifemelu is not wrong that she cannot force herself to feel offended; she can only choose to act offended if she understands that she is supposed to.

Because the experience of microaggressions is based on the accumulation of many small instances over a long period of time, they are often more contextual than more overt forms of racism. Ifemelu has, after all, encountered various situations that could also be termed microaggressions, especially during her relationship with Curt, that she has felt slighted by, like the salon that refused to do her eyebrows because they did not "do curly" (294). But it is clear that Ifemelu is much more sensitive to microaggressions that target her right to have access to spaces and services than those that are rooted in her perceived exoticness, perhaps because she actually does feel foreign rather than like she is being made to feel foreign. As I discussed in the introduction, both nonwhite immigrants and African Americans have been historically positioned as perpetual foreigners, although through different means. But for an individual like Ifemelu, who continues to feel herself to be foreign, this designation is less of a slight. Ifemelu is, therefore, freed to a certain extent from the effects of some more subtle forms of racism because she has not been socialized to understand them as such.

Ifemelu is not unaware of the problem that arises from different definitions of racism. In the blog entry "Job Vacancy in America—National Arbiter in Chief of 'Who Is Racist,'" she satirizes the fact that "in America, racism exists but racists are all gone," drawing attention to the way that only the most virulent forms of racism can be used to classify someone as racist (315). Her point that "somebody has to be able to say that racists are not monsters" is purposefully provocative to her lay readership not because it is not true but because it can be uncomfortable for racists and antiracists alike. People who harbor racist sentiments are happy to be able to point at "thin-lipped mean white people in the movies about the civil rights era" in order to not have to look more closely at themselves, and antiracists might prefer racists be easily identifiable rather than looking like "people with loving families, regular folk who pay taxes" (315). Her tongue-in-cheek solution is that a new term be created, like "Racial Disorder Syndrome," that can have different categories of sufferers: "mild, medium, and acute" (315). Discourses that connect racism to psychology are numerous in the real world, of course (for an overview, see Roberts and Rizzo). Ifemelu's critique also echoes the title of Eduardo Bonilla-Silva's book *Racism without Racists: Color-Blind Racism and the Persistence of Racial Inequality in the United States,* first published in 2003 and with four subsequent editions, which addresses the issue that Ifemelu is identifying here in detail. The blog format allows readers who would not pick up Bonilla-Silva's more-than-300-page book to be exposed to similar, if much simplified, ideas by reading a less-than-150-word post.

But it is telling that this post is placed at the end of the chapter during which the hair-touching incident takes place. This placement highlights the unsteady relationship between the blog and Ifemelu's life, especially because the text does not always make clear when certain blog posts were written. As such, Adichie's placement of this particular blog post at the end of this particular chapter does more to complicate Ifemelu's authorial credibility than to reinforce it. Read through the lens of the chapter that precedes it, Ifemelu could be read as externalizing and generalizing a personal and internal confusion. Her own uncertainty as to what does or does not qualify as racist is troublesome because of its direct effect on her romantic relationship with a man whose goodness she is attracted to but also made insecure by. The satirical tone of the post allows her to come across as detached but exasperated, and it does not reveal her own uncertainty in the way that some of her other blog entries do.

As I have argued throughout this book, respectability politics and model-minority discourse are two sides of the same coin, and both can act upon immigrant and second-generation Black women. Ifemelu rejects model-minority discourse by refusing to separate herself from African Americans and by using her voice rather than exhibiting the "quiet restraint" expected of the model minority (Nguyen 147). Her various nontraditional life choices, like living with her boyfriend and wearing her natural hair, also work against both patriarchal familial expectations and mainstream American assimilationist expectations. But she finds respectability politics more difficult to escape, perhaps because Blaine, as the symbol of respectability, seems so logical: "His positions were firm, so thought-through and fully realized in his own mind that he sometimes seemed surprised that she, too, had not arrived at them herself" (314). It is true, after all, that the behaviors of individual Black people are projected onto other Black people and that a Black person with a platform of any kind is expected to speak for Black people as a group. But the fact that these expectations exist does not mean that they need to be accepted. And, crucially for this novel, the fact that they exist does not necessarily mean that they act upon all people the same way.

Ifemelu's particular sort of privilege, to be less invested in Black American respectability or Black American struggle than Blaine, comes to a head in relation to the protest that Blaine organizes in response to the racial profiling of a campus security guard with whom he is friendly. Ifemelu has a personal dislike for this security guard as a result of his slightly sexually inappropriate treatment of her (343) and chooses not to attend the protest in favor of going to a lunch for an acquaintance, a professor going on sabbatical. She knows him through a Senegalese professor, Boubacar, with whom she has become friends and of whom Blaine does not approve. It is implied that Blaine's disapproval is rooted in Boubacar's arrogance and general Frenchness, while Ifemelu connects with him as a fellow African. The novel describes Blaine's feelings as a "territorial dislike that was foreign to his nature" (340), and though Ifemelu might interpret this jealousy as romantic, asserting that her feelings toward him are "fraternal" (341), Blaine's antipathy is clearly ideological. The form of respectability that Blaine embodies is fairly particular to the British empire's historical sphere of influence, and Boubacar's combined Africanness and Frenchness offers a different and perhaps more self-indulgent way of life. Boubacar is not a bad influence because he might seduce Ifemelu sexually but rather because he might do so sensually, away from the upright behavior as well as physical and moral purity that Blaine strives for. When Blaine texts her to ask where she is, she lies, saying that she missed it because she was napping, and she notices that when he returns he is "a little emotional, as though it had been a personal triumph of his" (345). His sense of personal achievement in having led this protest indicates that he sees this as only partially about the wronged party, although he suggests that the event benefited the security guard: "I felt as if that finally gave him some real dignity back" (345). Blaine's righteousness is, after all, not just about doing the right thing but setting the right example.

When he does find out that Ifemelu lied about why she did not attend, he is hurt and outraged. His chastisement of her speaks to the larger symbolic value of this event in their relationship, as he accuses her of essentially dabbling in race rather than being truly shaped by it: "You know, it's not just about writing a blog, you have to live like you believe it. That blog is a game that you don't really take seriously, it's like choosing an *interesting* elective evening class to complete your credits" (346). She rightly picks up on the fact that this speech contains "a subtle accusation, not merely about her laziness, her lack of zeal and conviction, but also about her Africanness; she was not sufficiently furious because she was African, not African American" (346). Ifemelu argues that this accusation is "unfair," but the novel does not strongly suggest that she is correct. Indeed, earlier in the novel, she admits as much to herself when Blaine's sister Shan, who she actively dislikes, argues that she could not write her blog if she were not African: "If she were African American, she'd just be labeled angry and shunned" (338). Ifemelu's feelings are hurt, but she thinks, "It was true that race was not embroidered in the fabric of her history; it had not been etched on her soul," and her main grievance is that Shan did not say this in private but in front of friends. Instead, in this instance, this cleavage is left unevaluated from a political standpoint. Ifemelu wishes "it were an uncivil emotion, a passion like jealousy or betrayal," that causes this conflict (346), which arguably reinforces Blaine's claim. "It"—which Blaine leaves undefined and which can be read as encompassing a wide variety of ideas and investments—is not personal for her in the way it is for him. This is not to say that Blaine is positioned as a hero in their interaction; his unwavering investment in "the principle of it"—regardless of what "it" is—marks him as often naïve and unbending in a way that is out of step with reality. At the very least, it is easy to imagine him as an insufferable person to be around if you knew him in real life. In the face of Blaine's disapproval, Ifemelu is finally revealed as not having successfully joined him on the side of the righteous. She still lies, she still chooses her own comfort over symbolic acts of solidarity, she still has personal feelings about individual people that shape her behavior toward them. Her position as a blogger was personally fulfilling, but her fear that it comes with more responsibility than she truly wants is clearly valid.

It is significant, then, that this chapter detailing the fight that breaks their relationship (although they remain together for a long time after, due to their shared investment in Barack Obama) is closed by a blog post that reads as an act of appeasement toward Blaine, titled "What Academics Mean by White Privilege, or Yes It Sucks to Be Poor and White but Try Being Poor and Non-White." The lack of clear time association between the posts and events does mean that it could also be read as having been written during the period mentioned earlier, when she was worried about his influence on her writing, in which case it would serve more as a sign of the fault lines in their relationship that predate their actual confrontation. Either way, the post is overtly and straightforwardly didactic in nature: it is made up mostly of a conversation between Blaine, referred to as Professor Hunk, and another person, and it literally reproduces Peggy McIntosh's famous "White Privilege: Unpacking the Invisible Knapsack" antiracism exercise (347–48). This is a clearly uncomfortable fit for Ifemelu. The information within the post is correct, and she attempts a casual tone through rhetorical moves like referring to McIntosh as "a pretty cool woman" (347), but it is remarkably impersonal. It does precisely what she said she did not want to do: explain rather than observe. As such, her strange sort of freedom, which is the root of their conflict, is for her nevertheless undermined precisely because of the personal; while she feels no sense of inherent connection to every Black person she encounters, in the way that Blaine does or at least tries to, she does feel personally connected to Blaine specifically. Indeed, the issue of this feeling is a core difference between the experience of many Black immigrants and that of African Americans. It would seem absurd to feel connected to everyone in Nigeria on the basis of a shared racial identity. But African Americans are their own "imagined community," as defined by Benedict Anderson, within the larger imagined community of the United States. This creates at least the idea, if not always the fact, of solidarity, especially for a person like Blaine. His implicit belief in racial uplift, his "talented tenth" positionality, imbues him with a sense of responsibility that is the result of time, place, and identity. It cannot be forced, and as the novel suggests, it cannot be faked.

Ifemelu began her blog as an outsider looking in, but the longer she remains in the US, the more she becomes what I have referred to as an insider-outsider, one who is both a part and apart of American society. The novel's title speaks to this transformation; she becomes Americanah, which marks her as both American and Nigerian and as neither. It is, perhaps, this same position that she sees in Barack Obama, as it is reading his book *Dreams of My Father*, his writing that ties him most to his African heritage, that makes her a devotee. Blaine is also a "true believer" in Obama (357), though his belief might be more tied to Obama's symbolic value and respectability. But even Obama's presidency cannot save their relationship. Months after their fight about the protest, Ifemelu breaks it to Blaine that she is moving back to Nigeria. To him this discussion is out of the blue, but she planned it for months before telling him.

Significantly, this breakup is revealed very early on in the novel, three hundred pages before the relationship is explored in detail. As a result, the doomed nature of their romance is clear to the reader from its beginning, as is the idea of Blaine as fundamentally "good" (7). Ifemelu's transformation into insider-outsider becomes a site of self-awareness in a way that she ultimately finds painful. She is insider enough to have internalized many American norms but outsider enough to realize that she has done so and that it has not come naturally: "She said the word 'fat' slowly, funneling it back and forward, and thought about all the other things she had learned not to say aloud in America" (6). Despite her seeming success both professionally and personally, she finds that there is "cement in her soul . . . an early morning disease of fatigue, a bleakness and borderlessness" (6). After thirteen years in the US, she has achieved the immigrant dream only to realize that she does not want to be an immigrant at all. She feels compelled to return to Nigeria, "the only place she could sink her roots in without the constant urge to tug them out and shake off the soil" (6). But here, too, her longing is not just or even primarily about abstract ideas like Nigeria the nation-state; she cannot deny that her longing for her "first love, first lover, the only person with whom she had never felt the need to explain herself," Obinze, played a role in her homesickness (6). Perhaps the difference between Ifemelu and Blaine that could never be overcome was a fundamental difference in the flow of investment: for Ifemelu, everything begins with the personal, which then comes into contact with the political, social, religious, etc., whereas for Blaine, everything begins in the abstract, and the personal must be forced into a shape set out by it.

I read Ifemelu's decision to return to Nigeria, then, as a final rebellion against the constraints set up around her as an African woman immigrant in the United States. Her decisive refusal to submit to being a model minority or a respectable Black woman in America comes in the form of refusing to be a Black woman in America at all. The end of her relationship with Blaine, both emotionally when they fought over the protest and physically when she told him she was going back to Nigeria, is the result of her inability or unwillingness to become good and righteous like him. Her years of observation, as expressed through her blog, indicate that this lack of transformation is not the result of her rejecting something that she did not try to understand. Indeed, at every stage of her time in the US, Ifemelu engaged in againstness; all of her intimacy coexisted with distance—with her parents back in Nigeria, certainly, but also with both of her serious boyfriends in the US. In those relationships, she let herself be subsumed to a degree, taking on their lifestyles of casual wealth and intellectual asceticism respectively, but always with an internal distance, as if she was watching her life in the same way that she watched the world, so that she could write about it in her blog. The novel resolutely presents Ifemelu as a flawed character, one who is often selfish, confused, and emotional—human in a way that Black women are not supposed to be, lest they lose the moniker of "strong" (222) that is the greatest merit they receive.

What, then, can be made of the novel's depiction of different forms of Blackness? Does Ifemelu's return to Nigeria suggest that there can be no meaningful union between Black Americans and non-American Blacks? I do not think this is what the novel suggests, for a number of reasons. First, the novel purposefully does not try to establish Ifemelu as archetypical or representative of African immigrants. She is a specific, flawed individual with a distinct history, personality, and set of investments. Second, the novel suggests that solidarity between African Americans and Black immigrants does not have to depend on conflating their identities and ignoring their differences. At its best, Ifemelu's writing notes where there is meaningful overlap between African American and non-American Black experiences, such as in the entry where she notes the existence of colorism throughout the African diaspora (215–16) and acknowledges that non-American Blacks cannot opt out of the American racial hierarchy (222) but also refuses to accept that the American way—including the African American way—of doing things is the only way, through assuming the role of one who can tell America about itself precisely because she comes from elsewhere. In this context, perhaps solidarity requires the acknowledgment and acceptance of difference, of multiplicity, and of conflict.

Throughout their relationship, Blaine would tell Ifemelu that she was being "lazy" in her thinking if she did not agree with him. One such instance is particularly telling. Ifemelu remarks on being confused by the "unbending, unambiguous honesties that Americans require in relationships" (321). Blaine asks what she means, and she answers, "It is different for me and I think it's because I'm from the Third World. . . . To be a child of the Third World is to be aware of the many different constituencies you have and how honesty and truth must always depend on context" (321). Rather than consider why this might be her sense of things, he responds by saying, "That is so lazy, to use the Third World like that" (321). He is accusing her here of "using" the Third World because he is unwilling to consider how other lives and other contexts might reveal what he sees as absolute to actually be contextual. For a respectable man like Blaine, laziness is a cardinal sin; it is the least respectable way to be. But for Ifemelu, who did not grow up in the shadow of the American myth of meritocracy and its legacy of puritanism, who is led more by desire than duty and has never had the expectation that the world will function as it ought, Blaine's way of thinking is as incomprehensible to her as hers is to him, but she is at least willing to recognize it as a difference rather than a situation where one is right and one is wrong.

In America, Ifemelu knows that she must be Black. But she also does not have to stay in America. Yet her return to Nigeria, thirteen years later, reveals that even if she never fully became American, she was transformed by her time there. And this, too, need not be unambiguously good or bad, right or wrong. The novel uses Obinze's perspective to give an external view of how she has changed, in a way that foreshadows her experiences when she returns to Nigeria. He reads her blog and finds them to be "so American and so alien, the irreverent voice with its slanginess, its mix of high and low language, and he could not imagine her writing them" (374). While Ifemelu thinks of Obinze as the one person in the world who understands her implicitly, he finds insights into her life alienating rather than comforting: "Because he had last known her when she knew little of the things she blogged about, he felt a sense of loss, as though she had become a person he would no longer recognize" (375). He is both right and wrong here; they must relearn each other, certainly, but the novel asserts that they are meant to be together. Indeed, in the context of this novel's overt social commentary, it is possible to lose sight of the centrality of the love story, but I argue that this actually fits very firmly within the novel's broader themes. The nuanced nature of the human experience that this novel tries to foreground, particularly through the imperfection of Ifemelu's character, is once again made explicit through having her find her happily-ever-after with a man who must leave his wife, with whom he has a child, to be with her.

Ifemelu's return to Lagos demonstrates how, by becoming an insider-outsider in the US, she has also become an insider-outsider in Nigeria. She finds Lagos a sensory assault on her arrival, which gives her "a dizzying sensation of falling, falling into the new person she had become, falling into the strange familiar" (385). Perhaps strangely, it is only by returning to Nigeria that she fully becomes the "new" person she had been developing into during her time in the US. It is the return to the familiar that solidifies her transformation. Her friend Rayinudo teases her about this by calling her "Americanah" and saying, "You are looking at things with American eyes. But the problem is that you are not even a real Americanah. At least if you had an American accent we would tolerate your complaining!" (385). Her decision during her time in the US to keep her accent means that the more obvious trappings of the changes within her are not present for those around her. But she does have the most significant symbol of her position as an Americanah: "a blue American passport in her bag," which she knows "shielded her from choicelessness" (390). The socioeconomic reality of her legal status in the US is particularly emphasized in the novel through its contrast to Obinze's journey as an undocumented immigrant in the UK. The novel's critique of the US requires the acknowledgment of the privilege that a connection to it provides elsewhere in the world.[1] But it is not just the privilege of access that leaving makes Ifemelu come to value more. When she and Obinze finally reconnect, she tells him, "The best thing about America is that it gives you space. I like that. I like that

---

1. The novel contrasts Ifemelu's ability to gain her American citizenship, aided by her first American boyfriend, Curtis, with Obinze's inability to gain legal status in the UK.

you buy into the dream, it's a lie but you buy into it and that's all that matters" (434). Here, Ifemelu describes the US as a place steeped in "cruel optimism" (Berlant 3). The narrative of the US is its best and its worst quality; the lie that one believes can be valuable because of how one mobilizes it.

Yet Ifemelu does leave, does ultimately choose to defy what Berlant describes as "cruel optimism's double bind: even with an image of a better good life available to sustain your optimism, it is awkward and it is threatening to detach from what is already not working" (263). Ifemelu's life in the US was not working on an affective level, even if it was working in economic terms; despite the success of her blog, "all those readers, growing month by month, linking and cross-posting," she is filled with malaise (6). The decision to leave, then, involves her acknowledging the appeal of the US's orientation toward cruel optimism, to even be drawn to it, and to still choose the awkwardness and the threat, to leave it behind for the starker world of Nigeria.

In Lagos, Ifemelu meets other new returnees, mostly through the Nigerpolitan Club. Like her, many of them bear the aftereffects of being a foreigner elsewhere, which has resulted in their being a foreigner at home. This is particularly marked by what reads as "self-styled quirkiness" that in the US marked their Africanness but in Nigeria marks them as no longer truly local: "a ginger-colored Afro, a T-shirt with a graphic of Thomas Sankara, oversize handmade earrings that hung like pieces of modern art" (407). Among these fellow former expatriates, Ifemelu feels comfortable and is uneasy with that realization (409). The number of people in Nigeria that she can relate to has shrunk because she has lived elsewhere, just as the pool of people she related to in the US was smaller because she was from elsewhere.

The novel's depiction of Ifemelu's rocky return home serves to reinforce not the idea that one can never go back to where one came from but rather to suggest that it is possible to use what was learned while away to see home better and more clearly. Adichie does so through the continuation of Ifemelu's writing. While she is stifled by working at the women's magazine *Zoe*, she finds her voice again through writing her new blog, *The Small Redemptions of Lagos*. Here, too, she includes voices other than her own by including interviews and guest posts (421); nevertheless, the blog is shaped by her interests and sensibilities. Through this blog, the novel puts forward a compelling argument for Africans who live in the West to return: it asserts the value of bringing the skills gleaned elsewhere home to contribute to making it better. It could be read as a sort of ironic reversal of colonial practices; for Africans to go to the countries that have extracted so much from them and do some extracting of their own for the purpose of building more ideal versions of their homelands.

While the argument for this extraction in a business context is commonly made, Adichie here models the value of it in artistic and intellectual contexts as well. She is, of course, not the first. The independence-era generation of African writers like Wole Soyinka and Chinua Achebe certainly did so as well. Nevertheless, Adichie seems particularly interested in how this can be done well in the contemporary moment. The representation of the Nigerpolitan Club, for example, is purposefully satirical both in how it is described in the narrative and how Ifemelu writes about it on her blog, in which she uses the metaphor of a dish called "assorted" that contains "beef and chicken and cow skin and intestines and dried fish in a single bowl of soup" to describe life in Lagos itself in order to chastise her fellow returnees, and herself, for complaining about it (421). The key, then, is to bring the same curiosity to Nigeria that she brought to America; to see it as a place that deserves the same amount of attention, even when that attention is snarky. She tells Obinze of her blog, "I have big plans for it. I'd like to travel through Nigeria and post dispatches from each state, with pictures and human stories, but I have to do things slowly first, make some money from advertising" (436). Her vision is pragmatic but appreciative of her homeland in all its diversity. The homogenizing that she experienced in the US, perhaps, has led her to particularly long for the multiplicity and complexity of Nigeria.

The moment in the novel that suggests that Ifemelu has reached a meaningful level of self-actualization is in relation to her writing, not her relationship, although the novel ends with the reunion of Ifemelu and Obinze. During the period between the end of her affair with Obinze and the ending when he leaves his wife to be with Ifemelu, she misses him but "still, she was at peace: to be home, to be writing her blog, to have discovered Lagos again. She had, finally, spun herself fully into being" (475). The self-fashioning that this description celebrates is the result of Ifemelu's resolute dedication to doing what she thought was best for herself, even when it was impractical. It also grows from her insistence on the personal. With her blog in Lagos, she is able to truly lean into her desire to observe, not explain, writing posts that draw attention to the everyday beauty and absurdity of life in Lagos without didacticism but with a strong point of view. Her post about the government demolishing hawkers' shacks, for example, zooms in on a woman who is slapped by one of the men sent to do the demolition: "Later, her face is burning from the slap as she watches her biscuits buried in the dust. Her eyes trace a line towards the bleak sky. She does not know yet what she will do but she will do something, she will regroup and recoup and go somewhere else and sell her beans and rice and spaghetti cooked to a near mush, her Coke and sweets and biscuits" (474). She does not need to tell her reader what they must do to save the hawkers or explain to them why this is happening. Her job is simply to show them something that they may have seen before, but through different eyes.

In Lagos, Ifemelu can write differently. In a conversation on the phone with Blaine, he asks her if her new blog is about race, and she tells him, "No, just about life. Race doesn't really work here. I feel like I got off the plane to Lagos and stopped being black" (475). This conversation is perhaps the novel's final rebellion against the idea that American racial discourse is universally applicable. Ifemelu stopped being Black in Nigeria because different things structure life there. She was Black when she was in the US; that experience of race was real and affected her in real ways. But it also was not always her reality. Perhaps this means that Blaine's accusations toward her about relative detachment from race in America were partially correct, but the novel does not suggest that this is something she must apologize for.

Americanah is a challenging novel to North American sensibilities in a number of ways, many of which are intentional. The novel's metatextual elements strengthen its emphasis on the personal, and its preoccupation with race as something that is contextual and experiential is coupled with an individual coming-of-age story in order to create a work in defiance of the oversimplification that discourses of race can establish. The novel ends with an Ifemelu who has learned how to channel her againstness creatively; her intimacy with Lagos is actually enriched by her having spent so many years away. The state of being against that she, sometimes subconsciously, cultivated while living in the US makes her a good observer. At the same time, the novel's interrogation of Blackness through the eyes of one who becomes Black upon her arrival is made powerful by its simultaneous ability to represent the concrete reality and effects of race and racism and denaturalize them at the same time. This novel examines and rejects both model-minority discourse and respectability politics through its protagonist, who, despite America's best efforts, remains stubbornly and messily a sometimes Black, sometimes immigrant woman.

CONCLUSION

The Future of Immigrant Blackness

This book has been largely about insider-outsiders, people who have certain insights into communities and nations that they are a part of precisely because they are not, or are perceived as not, wholly a part of those groups. I think it is fitting, then, that I am writing this from the position of an insider-outsider myself. I am the Canadian-born daughter of two immigrants, one from the culturally Anglo-Caribbean but geographically South American country of Guyana and one from the tiny, French-patois- and English-speaking island of Dominica, a nation fated to be regularly confused with the Dominican Republic because of uncreative colonists. Where and when I grew up—Toronto, Ontario, in the 1990s—the normative form of Blackness was one rooted in the Caribbean, Jamaica most prominently. Canada does have historic Black communities that have existed for generations, especially in certain parts of Ontario and the Maritimes, many of whom trace their arrival back to the formerly enslaved who entered Canada from the United States (pre- and post-Independence), including as loyalists to the British during the American Revolutionary War and as refugees from the War of 1812. But in the public imagination and as a result of a combination of a domestic workers scheme in the 1950s and changes to immigration laws in the 1970s, the largest Black presence in Canada is Caribbean.[1] Like most families from the Anglophone

---

1. For those interested in reading more about Blackness in Canada, Rinaldo Walcott's *Black Like Who*, Dionne Brand's *A Map to the Door of No Return*, and George Elliot Clarke's *Odysseys Home: Mapping African-Canadian Literature* are good places to start.

Caribbean, we have people in New York and in London. I noticed that even in New York City, a space heavily influenced by immigration from the Caribbean, the experience of Blackness for my cousins was quite different. This childhood observation was reinforced as I became an adult, through both reading novels like the ones explored in this book and through seeing friends and family who grew up Black in Canada move to the US for school or work. Watching multiple streams of the African diaspora reconverge is incredibly interesting and, as this book suggests, often quite fraught. Yet it is also an incredible opportunity to witness the resilience of African legacies, the ingenuity of African people, and the diversity of African diasporic experiences. As an insider to African-diasporic identity and the experience of being the daughter of immigrants, and an outsider to living in the United States but located within its sphere of cultural influence, I believe my insider-outsider positionality offers me a useful vantage point from which to observe a context so similar to and yet different from my own.

I bring up the formation of Blackness in Canada to situate myself and to offer a useful contrast between contexts. Because post-immigration-reform Black migrants to Canada have not historically settled in large numbers in the areas with significant populations of multigenerational Black Canadians (although I myself currently live in one such area), the challenge of reconciling these disparate experiences has often been discursive rather than lived concretely by everyday people. The convergence of Caribbean and African immigrants and African Americans in the urban centers of the United States is a relatively unique cultural and political context that is a fruitful site of both literary production and sociological inquiry. This book has taken up the task of exploring how a small but important selection of Black women writers have addressed this phenomenon.

The novels I have explored span several decades during which massive political, cultural, economic, and technological changes took place both within the United States and in the ancestral homelands of the writers. These novels are largely situated on the East Coast of the US, especially around New York and New England, not least because these areas are historical and present hubs of several Black immigrant communities. Of course, there are other such hubs, including in Florida, Minnesota, Michigan, and Texas, but these areas have not yet established as significant a literary footprint, although they may well in the future. Similarly, this book's engagement with African immigrant and second-generation writers is limited to West Africans because of their relative dominance in the literary landscape,[2] although the success of

---

2. Other significant West African American writers include Yaa Gyasi, Akwaeke Emezi, Chika Unigwe, Imbole Mbue, and Sefi Atta.

Southern and East African writers like NoViolet Bulawayo, Maaza Mengiste, and Meron Hadero hopefully signal an increase in the range of perspectives present in the literary scene. Factors including Southern Africa's history of settler colonialism and apartheid and East Africa's greater integration with the sphere of culture centered around the Indian Ocean rather than the Atlantic, as well as both regions' different relationship with the transatlantic slave trade in comparison to West Africa, produce their own complex relationships with race, culture, and indigeneity that undergo their own transformations through migration. There is much in this book that speaks to these different contexts, but there are also particularities and interesting points of contrast within them that have not been covered here. In short, this book has certain limitations of scope as a result of aiming for depth over breadth, but with the hopes that future scholarship will expand on this work.

As I mentioned in the introduction, the presence and influence of Black immigrants and their children in the US has been significant, most publicly in the areas of literature, music, and activism. The incredible importance of the Caribbean to the development of hip-hop, for example, cannot be overstated. As the presence of Caribbean and continental African immigrants continues to grow, attention to this group has also increased. Important social science research like Yoku Shaw-Taylor and Steven A. Tuch's *The Other African Americans* offers vital context to Black immigration to the US and draws attention to many of the same themes and topics demonstrated in the novels this book takes up, including the ways in which Black immigrants have been framed as model minorities. Although he does not use that specific term, Shaw-Taylor identifies the way that Black immigrant success, in contrast to that of African Americans, has been read as cultural rather than structural (3–5), a hallmark of model-minority discourse. Along with considered sociological research and thoughtful fiction, public discourses have also sprung up about the relationship between African Americans and Black immigrants in the US, sometimes in concerning ways.

The rise of the ADOS movement, which refers to the American Descendants of Slavery, is a stark contemporary example. The ADOS Advocacy Foundation's mission is to seek reparations specifically for the descendants of chattel slavery within the United States, and they adamantly insist on seeing themselves as separate from and deserving of different consideration than immigrant Blacks, regardless of whether their country of origin is also a place where chattel slavery was practiced, such as the Caribbean and Latin America: "Ours is an experience defined by the unique, shared cost of multigenerational plunder. And as we stand in the shoes of our ancestors, we insist upon a specific group designation as essential to this undertaking" (ADOS

Foundation). While at the end of their mission statement, they do claim to being "fiercely committed to advocating for policies that eliminate the divides faced by Black Americans with immigrant backgrounds" and acknowledge "the lived experience of racism and discrimination among all Black people in America," the group's rhetorical emphasis on contrasting themselves with Black immigrants and their descendants has led to their classification as nativist and anti-immigration by their critics (Stockman). Because this movement has developed in the virtual world of social media, tracing its core beliefs is complicated, but the research done so far on it through an analysis of the ADOS hashtag on Twitter found that nearly 10 percent of tweets using the hashtag were explicitly nativist or anti-immigration (Linvill et al. 358), and one of the founders of the movement, Yvette Carnell, was previously on the board of "Progressives for Immigration Reform, an anti-immigration group that has received funding from a foundation linked to John Tanton, who was referred to as 'the puppeteer' of the nation's nativist movement by the Southern Poverty Law Center" (Stockman). The ADOS movement, then, seems invested in asserting not just the distinctiveness of African American experience but also the unworthiness of Caribbean and African immigrants to benefit from the country their ancestors suffered in the making of. This movement inaccurately presupposes a strict border between African Americans and the rest of the African diaspora; there is a particularly long history of movement between the US and the Caribbean dating back to the colonial period (Shaw-Taylor and Tuch 9), and the settlement of Africans formerly enslaved in the US in Canada, Liberia, and Sierra Leone, as well as movement back and forth between these locations, complicates their worldview as well.[3] By refusing to view themselves as meaningfully connected to the rest of the African diaspora, they reject historical reality in favor of a focus on current economic issues, particularly a fear of African and Caribbean immigrants "taking" jobs and resources that they want for themselves.

It is notable that in the *New York Times* article that brought the movement into mainstream discourse, several of the attendees at an ADOS conference respond to charges of nativism by specifically calling out the ways that Black immigrants self-identify; one argues, "Every other group when they get here goes out of their way to say, 'I'm Jamaican. I'm Nigerian. I'm from Somalia.' . . . But when we decide to say, 'O.K. We are a distinct ethnic group,' people look at that as negative," while another states, "If you ask somebody who is Latino

---

3. Ironically, Cornel West is quoted as having argued in favor of the ADOS movement by seeing them as heirs to the work of Martin Luther King Jr. and Malcolm X (Stockman). One might wonder if Malcolm X would be entitled to only half-reparations, by the movement's logic, as a result of his mother's heritage.

what is their heritage, they'll tell you they are Puerto Rican or Dominican or Cuban" (Stockman). These arguments speak to an uncertainty about the distinction between national identity and racial identity, but they also demonstrate a genuine degree of hurt feelings on the basis of how Black immigrants have defined their own relationship to African American community and culture, as well as the white supremacist hierarchy they have internalized. This book has been critical of the desire among Black immigrants to see themselves as separate from or superior to African Americans, as have the novels that I have explored throughout. This criticism is in service of a vision of mutual respect and solidarity among the diverse communities that make up the African diaspora, and for such solidarity to be possible, nativism and American exceptionalism must also be rejected. The ADOS movement is young and its numbers small, but its volume and its online presence make directly addressing it necessary in this context.

In a strange way, the movement exists as a sort of funhouse mirror version of the argument of this book. This book and the members of ADOS agree that there are differences between the histories and experiences of African Americans and Black immigrants who reside in the United States and that Black immigrants are not more successful than African Americans because of a supposed cultural superiority. But this book argues that the ultimate winners in pitting these two groups against each other are white supremacists and American racial capitalism. Based on the targets of their activism, the members of the ADOS movement, on the other hand, seem to believe that the greatest threats against them and their economic well-being in the contemporary moment are immigrants, not capitalism.[4] Having fully accepted the value of capitalist competition, they seem to believe that their progress must come at the expense of the opportunities available to other groups and that appealing to white-dominated systems of power will be more successful if they are aligned with them against ethnic outsiders. In other words, they use the acknowledgment of real cleavages and conflicts between different African diasporic experiences and communities as a cudgel against other people of African descent. I roundly reject this logic.

The current debates about Black identity within the US raise the question of the future of immigrant Blackness. The works of fiction that I have explored in this book present personal narratives; all four of the novels have

---

4. This extends beyond just Black immigrants. For example, one of the attendees to the ADOS conference interviewed in Stockman's article argued that Mexican immigrants made it difficult for African American construction workers to find employment in Los Angeles. This laying of blame on immigrants for the decisions of employers is a classic example of anti-immigrant rhetoric.

at least some coming-of-age elements and emphasize the subjective experience of their protagonists. They neither try nor are they intended to present a totalizing view of immigrant or second-generation experience or a prescriptive view of the future. What they can do, however, is offer a space for genuinely engaging with the complexities and the possibilities of the present and the futures it might lead to. As readers of fiction, we are granted the privilege of seeing through eyes other than our own, eyes that can make the unfamiliar familiar and the familiar unfamiliar. Through this imaginative practice, envisioning solidarities and coalition-building across ethnic and national lines is made possible.

For this reason, I return to the concept of *against*. As I explained in the introduction, the power of the word *against* is that, unlike terms like *resistance* or *refusal*, it does not *only* signal the desire for distance. In everyday usage, *against* has two seemingly contradictory connotations: to be in opposition to something and to bring something near. These two directions serve as a grounding metaphor for the simultaneous push-and-pull relationship between the rebellious daughter and the world around her. The four novels discussed in this book all contain women characters who engage in some, often multiple, forms of *againstness* that show a resistance to various forms of control. These narratives demonstrate how Black immigrant and second-generation women's writing proposes a skepticism toward both familial and social control through the enforcement of respectability politics and model-minority discourse as well as toward nationalism and the misleading mainstream narrative of the US as a place of superior freedom for immigrant women.

Despite the significant differences in time period and national affiliation within the novels, each one depicted daughters who refused to simply accept the ways that they were supposed to be. *Brown Girl, Brownstones*' Selina and *Breath, Eyes, Memory*'s Sophie resist direct maternal domination, whereas *Ghana Must Go*'s Taiwo and Sadie and *Americanah*'s Ifemelu are more subject to broader social pressures than their individual mother's control; they exist more in the sphere of ambient social expectation, of which their individual mothers are only a part. At the same time, they are all also engaged in againstness in relation to the limitations and indignities that mainstream American society foists upon them. By identifying the ways in which gendered racism and racialized sexism, both in immigrant communities and mainstream US society, shape the lives of immigrant daughters, I have argued that these narratives of rebellion are not prescriptive but rather demand a recognition of why the need for rebellion emerges and the complexity of what it might look like to lay bare the many ways that discomfort demands ingenuity and imagination.

The rebellions explored in this book are shaped by what the character believes herself to be rebelling against. Because these characters are often coming of age, their sense of what they should be rejecting changes significantly throughout their lives. As such, many of the novels depict two stages of rebellion: one against an obvious target, usually a parent, and one against a more amorphous but more significant enemy, often systemic forces. This structure is valuable because it draws a connection between the personal and the structural for the reader, as the character also comes to recognize that these systemic forces shape their parents' behavior too. This realization does not necessarily absolve the parents of the hurt that they have caused, but it does model a kind of intergenerational understanding outside of the text even if it is not achieved within it. Sophie, Taiwo, and Sadie all initially rebel in ways that cause themselves pain because they believe it will save them from what feel like intolerable circumstances; it is only by coming to understand the suffering of their own mothers, rooted in colonialism and sexual violence, that they are able to enact their second rebellions, rebellions based on truth-telling, to themselves and to others. Selina's first rebellion against her mother is at first pleasurable, but a direct experience of racism forces her to reconsider her plan. Crucially, her newfound understanding does not lead her to submit to her mother's control but to enter the world with a clearer sense of what she is up against. Selasi's novel is the only one in which the end of the novel depicts a full reconciliation between mother and daughters, but it also includes a future in which they are separated by an ocean; Taiwo and her mother's renewed psychic closeness and Sadie and her mother's more adult relationship involve a healthy physical distance. In *Americanah*, Ifemelu also goes through a two-step process, although it takes a different shape than the others because she immigrates as a young adult. She also rebels against her parents by not living by their rules while she is abroad (and when she moves back to Nigeria), but the narrative focus is stronger on her several rebellions against systemic forces of racial, class-based, and gendered expectation as they manifest in the personal, particularly in her romantic relationships. These depictions of multiple rebellions speak to how life stages shape one's understanding and experience of racialization and gender construction, and the fact that the experience of these processes is not necessarily simultaneous with the cognition of them.

This book has demonstrated an investment in thinking across difference. The impulse behind this approach is inherently political insofar as it is predicated on a desire to construct a form of solidarity across individuals and communities that recognizes difference but also sees difference as neither absolute nor necessarily based on unchanging and static cultural identities. By reading across difference and seeking to find shared preoccupations and strategies, this project has tried to recognize linkages that can be further pursued both in literature and in lived experience. If, as I have suggested, Black women writers' representation of Black immigrant and second-generation positionality in the US demonstrates the unstable nature of racial categories and social hierarchies, then this literature can be seen as taking part in the larger social project of negotiating a worldview that takes an ethical, productive, and anti-essentialist approach to differences and creating space for connection and coalition-building. In "New Ethnicities," Stuart Hall argues for

> a recognition that we all speak from a particular place, out of a particular history, out of a particular experience, a particular culture, without being contained by that position as "ethnic artists" or film-makers. We are all, in that sense, ethnically located and our ethnic identities are crucial to our subjective sense of who we are. But this is also a recognition that this is not an ethnicity which is doomed to survive, as Englishness was, only by marginalizing, dispossessing, displacing and forgetting other ethnicities. This precisely is the politics of ethnicity predicated on difference and diversity. (227)

While Hall is writing about the UK context, his argument rings true for the emergent identities in the US as well. These new ethnicities, then, are not meant to usurp the place of nationalist identities, engaging in their same rapacious tactics, but rather to reimagine altogether how ethnicity and community interact. In grappling with what it means to be Black in the US—particularly in specific regions and contexts—and to have a specific ethnic or national identity along with that, these novels insist that specificity does not require competition or the denigration of others and that the lived experience of being "both/and" can be embraced rather than looked upon with suspicion. When Ifemelu chastises her fellow non-American Blacks for being obsessed with differentiating themselves from African Americans (Adichie 222), the text is not arguing that they should or even could eschew their preexisting identities based in nation, community, class, or country but rather that they recognize the political reality that makes it necessary for them to be in solidarity with African Americans. None of these novels suggest that such solidarity is natural or easy, but they do assert that it is vital.

The Black immigrant and second-generation women writers whose texts this book explores demonstrate an investment in this project of examining the tension between being ethnically located and refusing a kind of ethnic specificity that restricts the possibility of engaging across ethnic identities. Hall acknowledges that this project is difficult but necessary:

This does not make it any easier to conceive of how a politics can be constructed which works with and through difference, which is able to build those forms of solidarity and identification which make common struggle and resistance possible but without suppressing the real heterogeneity of interests and identities, and which can effectively draw the political boundary lines without which political contestation is impossible, without fixing those boundaries for eternity. It entails the movement in black politics, from what Gramsci called the "war of manoeuvre" to the "war of position"—the struggle around positionalities. ("New Ethnicities" 225)

An emphasis on position signals the contextual nature of identity. As I argued in the introduction, the novels I have discussed here are oriented toward a politics of identification rather than a politics of identity. A politics of identification allows one to come to understand how the processes of racialization and exclusion that Black immigrants and their children experience are reflective of "understandings of the material and ideological basis of all oppressions in their global manifestations; of the interconnectedness as well as the specificity of each oppression. And it is only meaningful if we develop a practice to challenge and combat them all" (Brah 104). These novels demonstrate that Black immigrants do not need to embrace a false homogeneity on the basis of race in order to resist the idea that they can improve their own lot by setting themselves above African Americans.

Through their protagonists, the novels also often question the psychological value of being accepted by the nation even as they are cognizant of the incredible social and political value of citizenship. National belonging is revealed to be both desirable and repulsive because gaining access to the nation-state's power structure and institutions often requires a performance of not only the "right" kind of national identity but also the "right" kind of ethnic identity. The ideological job of the immigrant, from the point of view of those in power, is to reinforce the idea of the nation-state as plural and benevolent, but the role of specifically anti-Black racism in American society constantly undermines this image. The immigrant daughters' position as, to a degree, outsiders to the culture allows them to see the host culture with a kind of clarity that is achieved by having to come to understand a place without the aid of native-born parents. As George Lipsitz argues,

> the populations best prepared for cultural conflict and political contestation in a globalized world economy may well be the diasporic communities of displaced Africans, Asians, and Latin Americans created by the machinations of world capitalism over the centuries. These populations, long accustomed

to code switching, syncretism, and hybridity may prove far more important for what they possess in cultural terms than for what they appear to lack in the political lexicon of the nation state. (30–31)

Here, Lipsitz is referencing not just post-1965 immigrants but the long-standing diasporic populations built by the forced migration involved in slavery, indenture, and colonization, but it is undoubtedly the case that the intergenerational difference I have described brings these practices of adaptation and interpretation into particularly sharp relief. The limitations of the nation-state are all the more visible despite the fact that the nation-state's power is also particularly evident through the presence of the processes of gaining citizenship, the threat of deportation, and other ways in which the state asserts its control over immigrants' lives.

At the same time, these novels are actively critical of cultural and social practices within the characters' ethnic communities, including the dangers of purity cultures in both *Brown Girl, Brownstones* and *Breath, Eyes, Memory*, the pain of intergenerational silences in *Ghana Must Go,* and the classist construction of Nigerian American identity in *Americanah*, to name but a few. This suggests that an uncomplicated turn to ancestral cultures is no solution to immigrant and second-generation alienation. Even in *Americanah*, in which the protagonist returns to the homeland, her altered perspective fostered while she was in the US ultimately serves an important purpose in offering her a critical distance from what she took for granted previously. Among the other protagonists, the connection to the ancestral homeland remains important but is by no means simple: Selina discards one bangle that is associated with her Bajan heritage but keeps the other, signally her continued in-betweenness; Sophie must return to Haiti to mourn and understand, but not to live or to create a future for her daughter; and Taiwo and Sadie are helped by the events of their trip to Ghana but must return to their messy lives in the US to apply what they have learned. Connection to the homeland remains vital but cannot be read as offering a simple escape from the complexity of racialization within the US.

The popular discourse about second-generation subjects is that they are "caught between two worlds," as if the solution is to choose one world to which they can fully commit or as if they simply cannot access one or the other. The texts analyzed in this book and others like them make clear that the multiple worlds (rarely just two) that the daughters of immigrants inhabit are not simply inaccessible and that a choice between them is impossible because no single one of these worlds contains all that they want or need. As I stated in the introduction, multidirectionality is a core aspect of immigrant and second-generation experiences. A turn to the past is needed to contextualize the present, but the future cannot be bounded by the constraints of the past, whether the past of the ancestral homeland or the past of the site of settlement. The events of the characters' parents' lives in the ancestral homeland powerfully impact the lives of the protagonists, even when they have limited understanding of those events, and the history and structure of race in America profoundly shapes their experience, but an important part of the characters' final rebellions is a refusal to let these pasts overdetermine their future.

If both striving for belonging within the US and longing for an idealized homeland are inappropriate for the needs of Caribbean and African immigrant daughters, what do belonging and the future look like? If the family unit can reflect or even exacerbate social inequities, forms of harm, and regimes of control but can also offer spaces of understanding, empowering visions of the self, and grounding connections in the face of uncertainty, what role can the family play in navigating the particular complexities of twenty-first-century life in the US and elsewhere? The texts explored in this book suggest that these unresolvable tensions require an approach that is shaped by this unresolvability, not one that tries to eliminate it. The insider-outsider position of the immigrant daughter is not always comfortable, but it is valuable because it produces a vantage point from which a critical and creative view of the world is possible. In Chang-Rae Lee's novel *Native Speaker*, a text that is itself deeply interested in exploring the relationship between immigrants and African Americans, he explores the insider-outsider tension from the perspective of a Korean American man, through an almost prophetic address to the reader:

> I and my kind possess another dimension. We will learn every lesson of accent and idiom, we will dismantle every last pretense and practice you hold, noble as well as ruinous. You can keep nothing safe from our eyes and ears. This is your own history. We are your most perilous and dutiful brethren, the song of our hearts at once furious and sad. For only you could grant me these lyrical modes. I call them back to you. Here is the sole talent I ever dared nurture. Here is all of my American education. (320)

Despite the differences of race and gender, this quotation beautifully and ominously characterizes the insider-outsider position because it speaks to the intimacy that the children of immigrants have with America—an intimacy that makes their Americanness both undeniable and threatening because it is achieved even as they are denied full belonging within it. For Black immigrants and their children, this is compounded even more by their Blackness, as the version of the idea of the perpetual foreigner that is applied to African Americans is combined with the version of it applied to nonwhite immigrants.

The daughters of Black immigrants are born into a world that often does not serve their interests. The convergence of race, gender, class, sexuality, and migration status act upon their consciousness and their bodies in ways that make visible, to those who are willing to see, both the power and the arbitrary nature of these systems. In *Feminist Theory from Margin to Center,* bell hooks argues that Black women hold a vital place in the feminist struggle because we lack an "institutionalized 'other' that we may discriminate against, exploit, or oppress" (15). As such, "it is essential for continued feminist struggle that black women recognize the special vantage point our marginality gives us and make use of this perspective to criticize the dominant racist, classist, sexist hegemony as well as to envision and create a counter-hegemony" (15). In this book, I have argued that the Black daughters of immigrants share this special vantage point, even though they may well have, in certain contexts and spaces, relative privileges because of their classification as model minorities. Yet the unsteadiness and the context-specific nature of such privilege reveals it to be all the more arbitrary, and indeed the possibility of such privilege being revoked at the whims of those with power makes such privilege significantly less attractive.

These texts reveal the lie of the national romance. Much immigrant literature can be integrated into the nationalist narrative—immigrant struggles are part of what prove the immigrant's worthiness to belong. But literature depicting the rebellious daughters of immigrants shows that those immigrant struggles do not result in total acceptance and a place within the supposedly coherent, essentially benevolent nation-state. But more than working as documents of alienation, the texts examined in this book ask the question, what now? If the national romance is a fantasy, or rather a promise that cannot be fulfilled, how might the supposed heirs to it develop a different meaning for themselves, a different sense of their place? If the persistence of racial hierarchy and white-supremacist capitalist patriarchy makes the promises of immigration unattainable for Black immigrant families, especially the women in them, what counterhegemony might emerge?

I argue that it is here that *against* emerges as not just a metaphor but an ethical ground from which to relate to systems, groups, and structures. The intimacy implicit in *against* is necessary because, regardless of how she is perceived, the Black immigrant daughter is a family member, a citizen or resident, a lover or friend, a participant in the world around her. The oppositional resonance of *against* is necessary because that intimacy does not curtail but in fact facilitates a critical perspective on the families, nations, relationships, and world that she engages with. The purpose of this argument is not to suggest that this model is prescriptive; this is a book of literary analysis, not a manifesto. In everyday life, to live in a constant state of *againstness* may well be exhausting and unsustainable. But in the context of literary and other cultural works that explore the subjectivity of Black immigrant daughters, the ability to call on and mobilize *against* as an orientation is a powerful resource.

The stories that we tell ourselves and each other matter. The stories of rebellious Black immigrant daughters speak to the fact that race, gender, sexuality, class, and migration status shape and act upon human lives in deeply contextual and interlocking ways. Literary and cultural representations of how Black women and girls resist and navigate these forces, sometimes successfully, sometimes not, reflect the real world but also speak back to it and attempt to reshape it. These novels express a hope for a future that includes solidarity between Black immigrants and African Americans, a solidarity that is built on a politics of identification rather than identity. They create space for imagining a rejection of homogenizing racial discourses, one that can coexist with a robust, cross-ethnic coalition of people of African descent against white-supremacist capitalist patriarchy, a future beyond the discourses of the model minority and respectability politics as modes of mitigating harm and gaining a small piece of a fundamentally flawed pie. And that is a future worth holding close.

WORKS CITED

Adichie, Chimamanda Ngozi. *Americanah*. Knopf, 2013.

ADOS Foundation. "Mission Statement." *Adosfoundation.org*, accessed 30 Aug. 2023.

Ahmed, Sara. "Being in Question." *Feministkilljoys.com*, 1 Apr. 2014.

Ahmed, Sara. *The Promise of Happiness*. Duke UP, 2010.

Alexander, Simone A. James. *African Diasporic Women's Narratives: Politics of Resistance, Survival, and Citizenship*. UP of Florida, 2014.

Anderson, Benedict. *Imagined Communities: Reflections on the Origin and Spread of Nationalism*. Verso, 2006.

Berlant, Lauren. *Cruel Optimism*. Duke UP, 2011.

Bhabha, Homi K. *The Location of Culture*. Routledge Classics, 2004.

Bonilla-Silva, Eduardo. *Racism without Racists: Color-Blind Racism and the Persistence of Racial Inequality in the United States Sixth Edition*. Rowman and Littlefield, 2021.

Boyce Davies, Carole. *Black Women, Writing and Identity: Migrations of the Subject*. Routledge, 1994.

Brah, Avtar. *Cartographies of Diaspora*. Routledge, 1996.

Brand, Dionne. *The Map to the Door of No Return*. Vintage Canada, 2001.

Butler, Judith. *The Psychic Life of Power: Theories in Subjection*. Stanford UP, 1997.

Christian, Barbara. *Black Women Novelists: The Development of a Tradition, 1892–1976*. Greenwood Press, 1980.

Chua, Amy. *The Triple Package: How Three Unlikely Traits Explain the Rise and Fall of Cultural Groups in America*. Penguin, 2014.

Clarke, George Elliot. *Odysseys Home: Mapping African-Canadian Literature*. U of Toronto P, 2002.

Cobb, Michael L. "Irreverent Authority: Religious Apostrophe and the Fiction of Blackness in Paule Marshall's *Brown Girl, Brownstones.*" *University of Toronto Quarterly,* vol. 2, no. 2, 2003, pp. 631–48.

Counihan, Claire. "Desiring Diaspora: 'Testing' the Boundaries of National Identity in Edwidge Danticat's *Breath, Eyes, Memory.*" *Small Axe,* no. 37, 2012, pp. 36–52.

Danticat, Edwidge. *Breath, Eyes, Memory.* Vintage Books, 1994.

Davis, Richard. *Typing Politics: The Role of Blogs in American Politics.* Oxford UP, 2009.

Dayan, Joan. "Erzulie: A Women's History of Haiti." *Caribbean Literature,* special issue of *Research in African Literatures,* vol. 25, no. 2, summer 1994, pp. 5–31.

Du Bois, W. E. B. *The Souls of Black Folk.* Oxford UP, 2007.

Echeverria-Estrada, Carlos, and Jeanne Batalova. "Sub-Saharan African Immigrants in the United States." *Migration Policy Institute,* 6 Nov. 2019, https://www.migrationpolicy.org/article/sub-saharan-african-immigrants-united-states-2018?gclid=EAIaIQobChMI75Dkq-Ca6gIVjZOzCh3beAqrEAAYASAAEgKn9vD_BwE.

Espiritu, Yến Lê. *Body Counts: The Vietnam War and Militarized Refugees.* UC Press, 2014.

Fahs, Breanne, et al. *The Moral Panics of Sexuality.* Palgrave, 2013.

Fan, Christopher T. "Battle Hymn of the Afropolitan: Sino-African Futures in *Ghana Must Go* and *Americanah.*" *Journal of Asian American Studies,* vol. 20, no. 1, 2017, pp. 69–93.

Foucault, Michel. "The Subject and Power." *Foucault: Beyond Structuralism and Hermeneutics,* edited by H. Dreyfus and P. Rabinow, U of Chicago P, pp. 208–26.

Francis, Donnette A. "Silences Too Horrific to Disturb: Writing Sexual Histories in Edwidge Danticat's *Breath, Eyes, Memory.*" *Research in African Literatures,* vol. 35, no. 2, 2004, 75–90.

Gerber, Nancy F. "Binding the Narrative Thread: Storytelling and the Mother-Daughter Relationship in Edwidge Danticat's *Breath, Eyes, Memory.*" *Journal of the Association for Research on Mothering,* vol. 2, no. 2, pp. 188–99.

Gilroy, Paul. *There Ain't No Black in the Union Jack.* Routledge, 2002.

Green, Tara T. "When the Women Tell Stories: Healing in Edwidge Danticat's *Breath, Eyes, Memory.*" *African American Fiction Since 1970: Critical New Essays,* edited by Dana A. Williams, The Ohio State UP, 2009, pp. 82–98.

Hall, Stuart. "New Ethnicities." *The Post-Colonial Studies Reader.* Routledge, 1995, pp. 223–27.

Harbawi, Semia. "Against All Odds: The Experience of Trauma and the Economy of Survival in Edwidge Danticat's *Breath, Eyes, Memory.*" *Wasafiri,* vol. 23, no. 1, 2008, pp. 38–44.

Heinrichs, Jürgen. "Primitivism." *Encyclopedia of the Harlem Renaissance,* edited by Cary D. Wintz and Paul Finkelman, Taylor and Francis, 2004, p. 992.

Hill Collins, Patricia. *Black Feminist Thought.* 2nd ed., Routledge, 2009.

Hirsch, Marianne. "The Generation of Postmemory." *Poetics Today,* vol. 29, no. 1, spring 2008, pp. 103–28.

Holloway, Karla F. C. *Legal Fictions: Constituting Race, Composing Literature.* Duke UP, 2014.

hooks, bell. *Feminist Theory from Margin to Center.* South End Press, 1984.

Hurston, Zora Neale. *Their Eyes Were Watching God.* Harper Perennial Modern Classics, 2006.

Ifatunji, Mosi Adesina. "A Test of the Afro Caribbean Model Minority Hypothesis: Exploring the Role of Cultural Attributes in Labor Market Disparities between African Americans and Afro Caribbeans." *Du Bois Review: Social Science Research on Race,* vol. 31, no. 1, 2016, pp. 109–38.

James, Winston. "Explaining Afro-Caribbean Social Mobility in the United States: Beyond the Sowell Thesis." *Comparative Studies in Society and History*, vol. 44, no. 2, April 2002, pp. 218–62.

Japtok, Martin. "Paule Marshall's *Brown Girl, Brownstones*: Reconciling Ethnicity and Individualism." *African American Review*, vol. 32, no. 2, 1998, pp. 305–15.

Jeffers, Asha. "'I Was Certain I Saw My Future in Him': Coming into Intergenerational Empathy and Escape in lê thi diem thuy's *The Gangster We Are All Looking For*." *Feminist Encounters*, vol. 6, no. 2, article 26, pp. 1–11.

Johnson, Jessica Marie. *Wicked Flesh: Black Women, Intimacy, and Freedom in the Atlantic World*. U of Pennsylvania P, 2020.

Kasinitz, Philip. *Caribbean New York: Black Immigrants and the Politics of Race*. Cornell UP, 1992.

King, Rosamond S. "Sex as Rebellion: A Close Reading of *Lucy* and *Brown Girl, Brownstones*." *Journal of African American Studies*, vol. 12, 2008, pp. 366–77.

Klein, Linda Kay. *Pure: Inside the Evangelical Movement that Shamed a Generation of Young Women and How I Broke Free*. Atria Books, 2018.

Lee, Chang-Rae. *Native Speaker*. Riverhead Books, 1995.

Lee, Jennifer, and Min Zhou. "The Success Frame and Achievement Paradox: The Costs and Consequences for Asian Americans." *Race and Social Problems*, 2014, vol. 6, no. 1, pp. 38–55.

Linvill, Darren L., Will J. Henderson, and SaiDatta Mikkilineni. "Divisive Social Movement on Social Media: Examining #ADOS." *Southern Communication Journal*, vol. 86, no. 4, pp. 349–61.

Lipsitz, George. *Dangerous Crossroads*. Verso, 1994.

Lowe, Lisa. *Immigrant Acts: On Asian American Cultural Politics*. Duke UP, 1996.

Marshall, Paule. *Brown Girl, Brownstones*. 1959. Dover Publications, 2009.

Masse, Michelle. *In the Name of Love: Women, Masochism, and the Gothic*. Cornell UP, 1992.

McGill, Lisa D. *Constructing Black Selves*. New York UP, 2005.

Millard, Kenneth. *Coming of Age in Contemporary American Fiction*. Edinburgh UP, 2007.

Miyares, Ines M., and Christopher A. Airriess. *Contemporary Ethnic Geographies in America*. Rowman and Littlefield Publishers, 2007.

Mohanty, Chandra Talpade. "Under Western Eyes: Feminist Scholarship and Colonial Discourses." *Feminist Review*, vol. 30, no. 1, Nov. 1988, pp. 61–88.

Morris, Susana M. *Close Kin and Distant Relatives: The Paradox of Respectability in Black Women's Literature*. U of Virginia P, 2014.

Nguyen, Viet Thanh. *Race and Resistance: Literature and Politics in Asian America*. Oxford UP, 2002.

Nietzsche, Fredrick. *Beyond Good and Evil*. Oxford UP, 1998.

Ninh, erin Khuê. *Ingratitude: The Debt-Bound Daughter in Asian American Literature*. New York UP, 2011.

Nnaemeka, Obioma. "Re-Imagining the Diaspora: History, Responsibility, and Commitment in an Age of Globalization." *Dialectical Anthropology*, vol. 31, nos. 1–3, 2007, pp. 127–41.

Olwig, Karen Fog. *Caribbean Journeys*. Duke UP, 2007.

Phiri, Aretha. "Lost in Translation: Re-Reading the Contemporary Afrodiasporic Condition in Taiye Selasi's *Ghana Must Go*." *European Journal of English Studies*, vol. 21, no. 2, 2017, pp. 144–58.

Roberts, Steven O., and Michael T. Rizzo. "The Psychology of American Racism." *American Psychologist*, vol. 76, no. 3, 2021, pp. 475–87.

Selasi, Taiye. *Ghana Must Go*. Penguin, 2013.

Shaw-Taylor, Yuko, and Steven A. Tuch. *The Other African Americans*. Rowman and Littlefield, 2007.

Somolu, Oreoluwa. "'Telling Our Own Stories': African Women Blogging for Social Change." *Gender and Development*, vol. 15, no. 3, Nov. 2007, pp. 477–89.

Stockman, Farah. "'We're Self-Interested': The Growing Identity Debate in Black America." *New York Times*, 8 Nov. 2019.

Sue, Derald Wing, et al. "Racial Microaggressions in Everyday Life." *American Psychologist* vol. 62, no. 4, May/June 2007, pp. 271–86.

Tamir, Christine. "Key Findings about Black Immigrants in the U.S." *Pew Research Center*, 27 Jan. 2022, https://www.pewresearch.org/short-reads/2022/01/27/key-findings-about-black-immigrants-in-the-u-s/.

Troester, Rosalie Riegle. "Turbulence and Tenderness: Mothers, Daughters, and 'Othermothers' in Paule Marshall's *Brown Girl, Brownstones*." *SAGE: A Scholarly Journal on Black Women*, vol. 1, no. 2, 1984, pp. 13–16.

Ukpokodu, Omiunota N. "African Immigrants, the 'New Model Minority': Examining the Reality in U.S. K–12 Schools." *Urban Review*, vol. 50, no. 1, 2017, pp. 69–96.

Valenti, Jessica. *The Purity Myth: How America's Obsession with Virginity Is Hurting Young Women*. Seal Press, 2009.

Walcott, Rinaldo. *Black Like Who: Writing Black Canada*. Insomniac Press, 2003.

Wright, Michelle M. *Becoming Black: Creating Identity in the African Diaspora*. Duke UP, 2004.

Zong, Jie, and Jeanne Batalova. "Caribbean Immigrants in the United States." *Migration Policy Institute*, 13 Feb. 2019, https://www.migrationpolicy.org/article/caribbean-immigrants-united-states-2017.

INDEX

Adichie, Chimamanda Ngozi, 2, 10, 28, 105
ADOS Advocacy Foundation, 132
African American women, diversity of, 22. *See also* Black women writers
African-diasporic literature. *See* Black immigrant literature
Africans, historical placement of, 7
against: as act of rejection, 54; duality of, 8–9, 53, 96, 135; intimacy of, 124, 141; metaphorical meaning, 4; transformative power of, 52
Agamben, Giorgio, 62
Ahmed, Sara, 9, 47
American Descendants of Slavery (ADOS) movement, 132–34
American racialization, 78
Americanah (Adichie), 2, 28, 105–29, 139
Anderson, Benedict, 123
anti-Black racism, 13. *See also* racial hierarchies
anti-Haitian sentiments, 59, 60
Asian North American women writers, 18

Battle Hymn of the Tiger Mother (Chua), 14

Berlant, Lauren, 80
Black Feminist Thought (Hill Collins), 22
Black identity debates, 134
Black immigrant literature, 3, 12, 13, 101, 132, 137, 141
Black women writers: on mother-daughter relationships, 19; and politics of representation, 9–10; portrayals of familial relationships, 19, 57; repoliticization of Black immigrant family discourses, 17; representation of Black immigrants, 137; and respectability discourses, 12; on respectability politics, 18–19
Blackness: African American experience, 5; in Canada, 130–31; forms of, 124–25; interrogation of, 129; and narratives of migration, 13; as racial construct, 2, 6, 42; as tool of white supremacy, 3, 111–12
blogs: origins of, 107; participation of African women in, 108, 110–11; as platforms for public discourse, 107–9; political nature of, 109; representation of Black women, 110
Body Counts (Espiritu), 78
body image, self-perception of, 99–100
Boyce Davies, Carol, 3, 6, 27

Brah, Avtar, 17, 25
Breath, Eyes, Memory (Danticat), 1, 2, 10, 27, 55, 56–76, 106, 135, 139
Brown Girl, Brownstones (Marshall), 2, 10, 27, 30–55, 106, 135, 139
bulimia as form of rebellion. *See* self-harm rebellion
Butler, Judith, 24–25

capitalist fatalism, 34, 40–41, 84
Carnell, Yvette, 133
Christian, Barbara, 31, 32, 52
Chua, Amy, 14
coalition building, cross-ethnic, 16–17, 135, 137, 142
colonialism, injustices of, 81, 82–83
coming-of-age: of daughters of immigrants, 2, 3, 4; multidirectionality of experience, 26; narratives of, 24, 25–26, 28, 78; physical transformation, 49; process of, 25–26, 28, 39, 105; and subject formation, 24–25
Counihan, Clare, 73

Dangarembga, Tsitsi, 96
Danticat, Edwidge, 1, 2, 10, 27, 55
daughters of immigrants: controlling bodies of, 18, 19, 37–38, 62–63; debt-bound, 18; definition of, 2; navigating family dynamics, 76; rebellion as resistance to respectability paradox, 18; relationships with mothers, 32; vantage point of marginality, 141
Davis, Richard, 108–9
Dayan, Joan, 71
debtor-creditor relationship, 17–18, 52, 56, 67, 92, 114. *See also* filial obligation
DiAngelo, Robin, 45
discourses on immigrants/immigration, 9, 13
Dreams of My Father (Obama), 123

Erzulie (goddess of love), 71–73
Espiritu, Yến Lê, 78
ethnography as immigrant experience, 8, 112

familial conflicts, 1, 12, 31, 57, 61
Fan, Christopher T., 114

feminist analysis on Western superiority, 20
Feminist Theory from Margin to Center (hooks), 141
filial obligation, 17–18, 36, 52, 56
foreigner positions of immigrants, 13–14
foreignness, freedom in, 118–19
Francis, Donnette, 73

gender dynamics of immigrant families, 31
Gerber, Nancy, 73
Ghana Must Go (Selasi), 28, 77–104, 106, 135, 139

Hall, Stuart, 137
Harbawi, Semia, 73
Hill Collins, Patricia, 21, 22, 23
Hirsch, Marianne, 46
hooks, bell, 141
Hurston, Zora Neale, 10, 115

immigrant families: expectations of compensation, 57; filial guilt, 62; gender dynamics of, 31; intersections of, 3; lack of mutual understanding of experiences, 103; language of silence, 78, 80–81, 82, 85, 96; perfection performance, 88, 89; as production units, 35–36, 84, 102; strained relationships within, 57
immigrant fiction, themes of, 1, 12
immigrants: and capitalist fatalism, 34, 40–41, 84; and coalition-building, 16–17, 135, 137; and conscription into Blackness, 117; and debt-bound familial relationships, 18, 114; and designated failure in familial discourse, 17–18; diversity of experiences of, 10, 131; double consciousness of, 100; as ethnographers, 8, 112; and filial obligation, 17–18, 36, 52, 56, 64, 66, 114; first-generation, 31, 40; and identity reformation, 116, 129; influence of, in US, 132; and masculinity, 38–39, 40; media representation of, 9, 59, 60; and merger opportunities, 13–14; and model-minority discourse, 14–16, 18, 34, 35; multidirectionality in narratives of, 26–27, 139–40; and national belonging, 138; national discourse on, 9, 141; navigating white supremacy, 8; nonrepresentative nature of, 7; ostracization of, 59;

and politics of respectability, 10, 34; and racial hierarchy acceptance, 8, 49, 113; and relationality of group histories, 21; and return to ancestral homeland, 106, 124; and sacrifices by mothers, 51; and separation of Black communities, 134; and unbelonging, 34, 40; and US citizenship, 5, 22, 126

immigrants, Asian American: and model-minority discourse, 14–16; model minority internalization, 15–16; narratives of generational conflicts, 12; as production units, 16

immigrants, Caribbean: Barbadian (Bajan), 31, 33; Haitian, 55, 59; and migration, 5; and model-minority discourse, 14; and racial hierarchies, 7; and respectability and class identity, 8, 10

Immigration and Nationality Act (1952), 5

immigration legal shifts, 5

immigration patterns, 4–5

Immigration Reform Act (1965), 5

Ingratitude (Ninh), 17

interethnic solidarity, 67, 70

intergenerational conflict, 1, 12, 17, 28, 101

intergenerational trauma. *See* intergenerational conflict

interracial relationships, 111–12

Johnson, Jessica Marie, 75

King, Rosamond, 49

kyriarchy, 19, 63

Lee, Chang-Rae, 140

Lee, Jennifer, 61

linguistic difference as tool of discrimination, 59

Lipsitz, George, 138

Lowe, Lisa, 12

Marshall, Paule, 2, 27, 30, 31–32, 54

masculinity, sense of, 38–39, 40

masochistic rebellion, 78, 79, 87, 91, 93, 94, 95, 97, 100, 102. *See also* self-harm rebellion

Masse, Michelle, 78

McIntosh, Peggy, 122–23

media representation, 9, 59, 60

merger opportunities for immigrants, 13–14

microaggressions, 119

migration: different contexts of, 132; gendered experience of, 26; historical placement of, 7; postslavery, 4; quota system, 4–5; statistics, 4–5; through enslavement, 4

Millard, Kenneth, 24

model minority: and capitalist fatalism, 34, 36, 40, 41; critique of, 49; as cultural identity, 94; discourses on, 14, 18, 34, 35, 84, 132; and glass ceiling, 34; internalization of discourses on, 61; origins of concept of, 14; rejection of, 120, 129; as tool to shame other minorities, 113

Mohanty, Chandra Talpade, 20, 115–16

Morris, Susana, 16, 18, 53, 83

mother line, 61, 68, 74. *See also* mother-daughter relationships

mother-daughter relationships: ambivalent nature of, 67, 68; confrontation dynamics in, 42, 98, 102; and cycle of trauma, 69; and gendered expectations, 58; power and influence in, 39, 56, 62–63; protection and punishment in, 84–85; and self-recrimination, 83; transformation of, 52–53, 74. *See also* debtor-creditor relationship

multidirectionality of immigrant narratives, 26–27, 139–40

National Origins Act (1924), 4

Native Speaker (Lee), 140

Nervous Conditions (Dangarembga), 96

New York Times, 133

Ninh, erin Khuê, 15, 16, 17, 35, 36, 37, 52, 56, 64, 78, 83

Obama, Barack, 123

Other African Americans, The (Shaw-Taylor & Tuch), 132

parental control, rebellion against, 30, 55, 61

paternal abandonment, themes of, 81–82

patriarchal familial dynamics, 20–21

Pew Internet and American Life Project, 108

Pew Research Center, 5
Phiri, Aretha, 96
positionality, 16, 23, 31, 61, 86, 114, 131, 137
primitivism, 48
production units, 16, 35–36, 84, 102

racial hierarchies, 8, 49, 113
racial identity in the US, 6
racialization, process of, 26, 138
racism, 31, 37, 39, 44, 49, 50
rebellion: against American racial discourse, 129; and deferral of accountability, 91; masochistic form of, 78, 79, 87, 91, 93, 94, 95, 96, 97, 100, 102; meaning-making as, 107; against parental control, 30, 55, 61; as performance, 89, 95; and process of freedom, 73–75; as resistance to respectability, 18, 51, 64–65, 73, 75; return to ancestral homeland as, 124; and self-destruction, 78, 91; self-harm as act of, 55, 64–65, 78, 86–87, 93, 96; and sibling connections and contrasts, 101; against silence, 67; stages of, 136
Refugee Act (1980), 5
relationality of group histories, 21
reparations, 132
respectability: and beauty standards, 89; and capitalist fatalism, 34, 87; characterization of, 35; critique of, 35; and liberal white racism, 45; paradox of, 18–19, 58; politics of, 10–12; rejection of, 44–45, 53–54, 55, 67–68, 129; resistance to, 18, 51, 64–65, 73, 75; and sexuality control, 63; social mobility as result of, 60
return to ancestral homeland, 106, 124, 126–27, 128, 139

sameness and difference, theme of, 32, 70–71
second generation: and Blackness, 16; caught between two worlds, 139; coming-of-age narratives, 26; and double consciousness, 100; and gendered expectations, 37; multidirectionality, 139; positionality, 16, 27, 86, 107, 137; and racialization, 27, 78; relationships with first generation, diversity of, 100; and women's liberation, 17; writing by, 1, 3, 4, 10, 17, 26, 27, 79, 104, 106, 131, 135, 137
Selasi, Taiye, 2, 10, 28, 77
self-harm rebellion, 55, 64–65, 78, 86–87, 93, 94, 96. *See also* masochistic rebellion
sexual violence, familial histories of, 66, 69
sexuality, control of, 61–62
Shaw-Taylor, Yoku, 132
silence, language of, 78, 80–81, 82, 85, 96
slavery: impact of, on migration, 4, 6–7
solidarity between Black communities, 9, 116, 125, 134, 136, 137, 142
Southern Poverty Law Center, 133
Sowell, Thomas, 14
spiritual elements, theme of, 71
subject formation, 24

Tanton, John, 133
Their Eyes Were Watching God (Hurston), 115
therapy as rejection of silence, 68–69
transnational solidarity, 22, 23
transversal politics, 21
tribalism in America, 105
Triple Package, The (Chua), 14
Tuch, Steven A., 132

"Under Western Eyes" (Mohanty), 20
US Black feminism, 22, 23, 24
U.S. News & World Report, 14

white fragility, 45
white supremacy, inescapability of, 50, 83
Wright, Michelle, 7
Wright, Richard, 10

Zhou, Min, 61

www.ingramcontent.com/pod-product-compliance
Lightning Source LLC
Chambersburg PA
CBHW020741230426
43665CB00009B/518